Wearable
Quilts

Wearable Quilts

Sewing Timeless Fashions Using Traditional Patterns

Roselyn Gadia-Smitley

 Sterling Publishing Co., Inc. New York

Apparel design and black-and-white illustrations by Roselyn Gadia-Smitley
Color photography by Nancy Palubniak
Edited by Isabel Stein

Library of Congress Cataloging-in-Publication Data

Gadia-Smitley, Roselyn.
    Wearable quilts: sewing timeless fashions using traditional
patterns / by Roselyn Gadia-Smitley.
        p.   cm.
    Includes index.
    ISBN 0-8069-8800-2
    1. Quilting.   2. Quilting—Patterns.   I. Title.
TT835.G33   1992
746.9′2—dc20   92-41341
                                            CIP

            4   6   8   10   9   7   5
Published by Sterling Publishing Company, Inc.
387 Park Avenue South, New York, N.Y. 10016
© 1993 by Roselyn Gadia-Smitley
Distributed in Canada by Sterling Publishing
℅ Canadian Manda Group, P.O. Box 920, Station U
Toronto, Ontario, Canada M8Z 5P9
Distributed in Great Britain and Europe by Cassell PLC
Villiers House, 41/47 Strand, London WC2N 5JE, England
Distributed in Australia by Capricorn Link Ltd.
P.O. Box 665, Lane Cove, NSW 2066
Manufactured in the United States of America
All rights reserved
Sterling ISBN 0-8069-8800-2

Contents

[Color illustrations are after page 64]

Preface

What is a wearable quilt? Simply put, it is a timeless fashion. A wearable quilt is a piece of wearable art with a unique style of its own that derives from an old tradition. Patchwork quilts had humble beginnings as bedcovers. More recently, they have become cherished antiques. In addition, the quilt has taken on a new role in clothing created as a decorative art form. The timeless beauty of the quilt has brought a new dimension to today's fashion.

By using your creative talents, you can create your very own wearable quilt. Minimum sewing skills are all that are required. As you master your skill, you can progress to more challenging projects. Let your personal style show in your quilt.

Creating a wearable quilt does not require you to go to a great deal of expense. Materials in the home, such as outdated clothing and remnants from previous sewing projects, are ideal for piecing a quilted garment. Be resourceful and use material you already have. To make your garment interesting, use varying prints and colors to accentuate the patchwork pattern. If you prefer, pick up sale-priced remnants from your local fabric store and incorporate them with compatible fabrics you already have on hand.

Whatever fashion trends may dictate, the classic styles in this book will remain timeless. The garments are especially designed to be adapted to any type of occasion, whether it be during the daytime or evening. Included in the book are: apparel patterns in grid form, full-sized patchwork patterns, and step-by-step instructions with detailed illustrations.

This book is intended as an instructional manual for the novice as well as a reference guide for the expert quilter. The projects range from simple, beginner's projects to advanced projects for the expert quilter.

Full-size patchwork pattern templates are given without seam allowances to facilitate precise tracing of the patterns. Add ¼″ (.6 cm) seam allowance around each template after you have traced it onto the fabric. Your template's tracing lines will serve as your sewing lines in the piecing of the quilt top.

Gridded apparel patterns are given in reduced form. You will need to enlarge these patterns. Apparel patterns also are given without seam allowances. Add ⅝″ (1.6 cm) seam allowances to your apparel patterns. These procedures will be described in detail later in the book.

The section "More Patchwork Patterns" includes 21 additional patterns that may be used with any of the apparel patterns in the book.

List of Terms and Symbols

Apparel pattern. A clothing pattern used in the construction of a garment.

Backing material. The lining of the quilt or quilted garment.

Batting. The middle layer of the quilt, which gives depth to the quilt. Batting materials include loose polyester and cotton fibres, bonded polyester fibres, and lofty woven materials such as flannel. Batting is available in several thicknesses.

Block or quilt block. A group of assembled patchwork pieces that form a unit of the quilt's design motif. Examples are the Sawtooth Block and the Churn-Dash Block.

Ground or background fabric. The top layer of the quilt, upon which patches or blocks are appliquéd or otherwise attached.

Hue. Another word for *color*.

Patchwork pattern. The pieced design used to form the quilt-top. Patchwork patterns may be formed by assembling patchwork blocks, such as Bow-Tie or Churn-Dash Blocks, or by assembling an overall pattern, such as Crazy Quilt.

Preshrinking. The process whereby fabric is soaked or washed to relax the fibres in place before it is cut or assembled. Preshrinking reduces the amount the garment will shrink after it is washed.

Quilting pattern. The quilting pattern is the stitching pattern used to quilt the garment. The pattern may be executed in running stitch or backstitch.

Quilt-top. The top layer of the quilt (the one on which the design is assembled).

Quilt-top fabrics. Fabrics used in piecing the quilt-top.

Wearable quilt. A quilt that is specifically designed as an article of clothing.

Symbols

CB Center of back.

WS Wrong side of the fabric.

RS Right side of the fabric.

↕ Place on the grain line or place parallel to the finished edge of the fabric (the selvage).

⌐ Place on the fold of the fabric.

Figure 1A. Horizontal and vertical lines.   *Left:* The use of horizontal lines widens the figure, but denotes a relaxed appearance.   *Right:* The use of vertical lines adds height and has a slimming effect.

1

Planning a Wearable Quilt

Planning the quilted garment is the primary step in creating your garment. Consider the fabric selection, the care of the garment, and the elements of design in planning your quilt.

Fabric Selection

In selecting fabrics, ease in handling and fabric durability are primary factors. Woven cottons and woollens are recommended materials for quilting. Aside from their durability and ease in handling, woven cottons and woollens will press down easily. Silk, linens, and synthetic fabrics are difficult to handle. On the other hand, an experienced seamstress may be able to work with these materials with relative ease. If you are experienced, do experiment with various materials.

When selecting fabrics, group them according to their fibre classification. Cotton patches should only be used with cotton patches. Similar types of fabrics will require the same type of care in laundering; mixing fabrics may cause laundering or unequal-shrinkage problems.

The creative individual, however, is not limited to woven cottons and woollens alone. Velvets, satins, laces, and other fabric types provide interesting textures and effects. Although novelty fabrics may not be suitable for everyday use, these can be incorporated into specialty-wear clothing such as evening wear and bridal gowns. Experimentation is a challenge to the creative quilter.

Use and Care of the Garment

Cottons and other washable materials can be washed gently by hand. To remove excess moisture, gently squeeze the quilted garment. Do not wring the quilted garment to remove moisture. The wringing motion can cause the quilting stitches to break. The garment can then be laid flat on a towel while it is dripping wet; thereafter it can be hung to dry. A sweater rack is also handy for drying a quilted garment. Woollens and silk

fabrics should be dry-cleaned according to instructions. If your fabric is newly purchased, you may find instructions on the fabric bolt. Dry cleaning will prevent dyes from running and also will prevent residual shrinkage of the fabric. The mechanical action of the dry-cleaning process will weaken the quilting stitches after several cleanings, so dry cleaning should be done only when it is necessary.

For storage, wearable quilts can be safely hung on padded hangers. If storing a quilted garment in a chest, make sure that no part of the wood is touching the quilt. Wood stains and oils can be picked up readily by the quilt, which may cause discoloring of the fabrics. To allow for air circulation, do not place excessive weight on top of your quilt. This will help you to avoid creasing the fabric also.

Elements of Design

The aesthetic appeal of a quilted garment is based on the elements of design: line, form, color, and texture. All these elements must be combined to form a harmony of balance and proportion.

Line

Lines measure and indicate shapes, leading the eye to specific directions. Line creates the silhouette of the garment. Line also implies certain meanings: straight lines are associated with strength and curved lines, with gracefulness.

Lines may be divided into four categories: vertical, horizontal, diagonal, and curvilinear. Manipulation of line creates the illusion of space. To create a desirable overall effect, carefully choose the lines emphasized for each garment. Review Figures 1A and 1B for guidance.

Lines can be manipulated to suit each person's individual needs, as follows:

Vertical Lines. Vertical lines are most suitable for petite and full-figured individuals. Vertical lines give height and are slimming (see Figure 1A, right).

Figure 1B. Circular and diagonal lines. *Left:* The use of circular lines is most effective when emphasis towards the face is desired. *Right:* The use of diagonal lines has a slimming effect, adds height, and imparts a sense of drama.

Horizontal Lines. Horizontal lines widen the figure and appear to shorten height (see Figure 1A, left). Horizontal lines are suitable for the slim and tall figure. Horizontal lines, however, evoke a relaxed and sporty appearance.

Diagonal Lines. Diagonal lines are flattering to almost all figures. Diagonal lines impart a slimming effect, height, and a sense of drama (see Figure 1B, right).

Circular Lines. Circular lines denote activity and place emphasis on certain parts of the body. The use of circular lines is most effective when emphasis towards the face or the upper part of the body is desired (see Figure 1B, left).

Form

Form is created when lines are combined to form closed shapes. Common shapes are squares, rectangles, triangles, and circles. Manipulation of these shapes within the wearable quilt is vital to the aesthetic appearance of the finished garment.

A garment divided into small shapes is desirable for the majority of individuals (see Figure 2, left). Large shapes within the garment tend to overpower the individual and, at the same time, add weight (see Figure 2, right). The traditional, large quilt blocks must be reduced to harmonize the appearance of the pattern with the height and weight of the individual. A common mistake is to use a bed quilt block to make a wearable quilt.

Unity of form is achieved by the similarity of shapes or repetition of shapes within the design of the garment. The shape of collars, for example, affects the unity of the design elements. Sharper collar points are required by angular fabric design lines; curvilinear fabric design lines require circular collar shapes (see Figure 3).

Color

Red, yellow, and blue are the primary colors, of which other colors are composed. Black, white, and brown are neutral media used to lighten or darken hues. When two primary colors are mixed together, a secondary color is produced. Secondary colors are green, violet, and orange. Mixing a primary and secondary color forms an intermediate or tertiary color. Tertiary colors are: red-violet, blue-violet, blue-green, yellow-green, yellow-orange, and red-orange (see Figure 4).

A color may be classified by its value and intensity. *Value* refers to the lightness or darkness of a color. This is changed by adding white or black to the color.

Intensity refers to the brightness or dullness of a color.

Light colors and bright colors have the same effect in a wearable quilt. Both light and bright colors tend to make the garment appear to advance. In addition, they appear to impart weight to the individual wearing the garment.

Dark and dull colors tend to make the garment recede, creating a slimming effect. However, when dark colors are used in segmented areas, they appear to impart weight to the portion of the garment in which they are used (see Figure 5). When dark and dull colors are used exclusively in a pattern, the result is an uninteresting garment.

Light, bright, dull, and dark colors produce the most interesting effects when they are combined in proper proportions. Color schemes may be based on monochromatic, complementary, or related color harmonies, as discussed below.

Monochromatic Color Scheme. A monochromatic color scheme is based on using only one color in various shades, tints, and intensities. A monochromatic color scheme is restful, but it can also become boring. When you use a monochromatic color scheme in a garment, you should choose accessories and cosmetics carefully to complement it. Jewelry with shiny surfaces will add interest to the total appearance of the garment, for example.

Complementary Color Scheme. A complementary color scheme uses colors that are opposite each other on the color wheel, such as yellow and violet. Complements may be used in various shades, tints, and intensities. Complementary colors like red-orange and blue-green create stimulating and interesting effects in patterns. The use of complementary colors is particularly effective when a dramatic, intense color scheme is desired (see Table 1).

Related Color Scheme. A related color scheme uses colors that are next to each other on the color wheel, such as red, red-violet, and blue. The use of three or more related colors produces interesting effects. A related color scheme causes subtle changes in color transition, especially when muted shades are used.

Related colors in the red, orange, and yellow range are classified as warm colors. Warm colors appear to advance and, at the same time, add weight to the wearer of the garment. To subdue the intensity of warm colors, use them as tints or pastels. Colors in the violet, blue, and green range are classified as cool colors; they tend to recede and therefore are more suitable for wearable quilts.

Accented Scheme. An accented scheme uses neutral tones as controlling colors and adds one or two hues as the accent of the composition. Neutral tones are black, white, brown, grey, and beige. A color coordination

Figure 2. Form.   The use of small shapes in the wearable quilt is vital to the aesthetic appearance of the finished garment, as illustrated on the left figure. Small shapes are better suited to the human figure.

Figure 3. Unity of form is achieved by repetition of shapes in the design and fabric of the garment. *Left:* Curved collar and sleeves are echoed by curves in the pattern of the fabric. *Right:* angular collar and sleeves complement the geometric fabric design.

TABLE 1.   COLOR COORDINATION CHART

Color	Complementary Color	Related Color Schemes	
Blue	Orange	*Warm theme:*	Blue, blue-green, green, yellow-green, yellow, orange
		Cool theme:	Blue, blue-violet, violet, red-violet
Blue-green	Red-orange	*Warm theme:*	Blue-green, green, yellow, yellow-orange
		Cool theme:	Blue-green, blue, blue-violet, violet, red-violet
Blue-violet	Yellow-orange	*Warm theme:*	Blue-violet, blue, blue-green, green, yellow-green
		Cool theme:	Blue-violet, violet, red-violet, red
Green	Red	*Warm theme:*	Green, yellow-green, yellow, yellow-orange
		Cool theme:	Green, blue-green, blue, blue-violet, violet
Red	Green	*Warm theme:*	Red, red-orange, yellow-orange, yellow, orange
		Cool theme:	Red, red-violet, blue-violet, blue
Red-orange	Blue-green	*Warm theme:*	Red-orange, orange, yellow-orange, yellow, yellow-green
		Cool theme:	Red-orange, red, red-violet, violet, blue-violet
Red-violet	Yellow-green	*Warm theme:*	Red-violet, red, red-orange, yellow-orange
		Cool theme:	Red-violet, violet, blue-violet, blue
Orange	Blue	*Warm theme:*	Orange, yellow-orange, yellow, yellow-green, green
		Cool theme:	Orange (pastel), red-orange, red, red-violet, violet
Violet	Yellow	*Warm theme:*	Violet, red-violet, red, red-orange, orange (pastel)
		Cool theme:	Violet, red-violet, blue-violet, blue, blue-green
Yellow	Violet	*Warm theme:*	Yellow, yellow-orange, orange, red-orange, red
		Cool theme:	Yellow (pastel), yellow-green (pastel), green (dark), blue-green, blue
Yellow-green	Red-violet	*Warm theme:*	Yellow-green, yellow, yellow-orange, orange
		Cool theme:	Yellow-green (pastel), green (dark), blue-green, blue
Yellow-orange	Blue-violet	*Warm theme:*	Yellow-orange, orange, red-orange, red
		Cool theme:	Yellow-orange (pastel), yellow (pastel), green (dark), blue-green

chart is included for simplification of color schemes (Table 1). Experiment with various tints and shades to find the most favorable result.

Texture

The surface quality or tactile feel of the fabric is known as texture. Napped surfaces such as velvets tend to add the appearance of weight to the individual. Shiny surfaces such as satins tend to advance the garment, thus adding visually to the physical size of the individual. Dull and smooth surfaces such as those of plain woven cottons tend to appear less in weight, making this texture the most desirable type to wear.

Wardrobe Coordination

In planning your wearable quilt, take into consideration your personal style, your color preferences, and the accessories available in your existing wardrobe.

Your personal style evolves from your preferences in life-style. Determine the quilted garments that you will need in terms of their function and durability for your life-style and activities.

Analyze your color preferences by examining your wardrobe. Notice the colors of the clothes you already own. You can analyze the color harmonies that you have already favored in your wardrobe by reference to the color wheel (Figure 4). Then you can plan your quilted garment to go with or spark the harmonies you already favor.

Wearable quilts are very versatile and can easily be worked into an existing wardrobe. A wearable quilt is an outstanding piece of clothing. Keep your ensembles simple by coordinating them around the quilted garment. In other words, treat the quilted garment as a printed fabric when planning your accessories and the other garments that you will wear with it.

Basic accessories include shoes, bags, belts, jewelry, and cosmetics. It is likely that you already have coordinating accessories that harmonize with your color preferences. Use simple accessories so that the other items in the ensemble do not compete with the quilted garment. The simplest method is to choose one basic color as the controlling color in the ensemble.

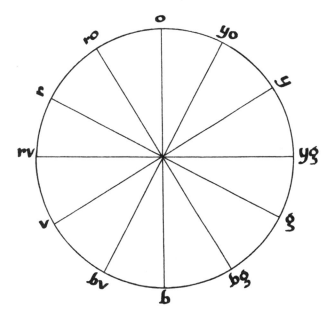

Figure 4. The color wheel illustrates the primary, secondary, and tertiary colors. Primary hues are red (r), yellow (y), and blue (b). Secondary hues are green (g), violet (v), and orange (o), which are products of the mixture of adjacent primary colors. Tertiary colors are red-orange (ro), red-violet (rv), blue-violet (bv), blue-green (bg), yellow-green (yg), and yellow-orange (yo), which are products of the mixture of adjacent primary and secondary hues.

Figure 5. When dark colors are used in segmented areas, they will impart weight to that portion of the garment. *Left:* The weight is placed in the upper torso. *Right:* The weight is placed in the lower torso.

2

Equipment, Patterns, and Material

The use of the proper equipment will greatly speed up the construction of your garment. The equipment and patterns that you will need are discussed below.

Equipment and Patterns

Patchwork Patterns

The patchwork pattern prescribes the surface design of the quilt. Patchwork pattern blocks and templates are drawn in this book without seam allowances. You therefore need to add ¼" (.6 cm) seam allowance around the templates after you trace them onto the fabric.

Apparel Patterns

Apparel patterns (patterns of garments) are diagrammed in reduced form in this book; they must be enlarged before you use them. After enlarging a pattern, adjust it to your specific measurements. The apparel patterns in this book do not include seam allowances. Add ⅝" (1.6 cm) seam allowances around the enlarged and adjusted patterns to get the cutting lines. This process is discussed in more detail in Chapter 4, "Enlarging and Adjusting an Apparel Pattern's Size."

Commercial apparel patterns may be used instead of the ones given in this book. When you choose a commercial pattern to make a wearable quilt, select one without darts, tucks, or pleats. If the pattern does not call for quilted fabrics (under the list of suggested materials), add ½" (1.3 cm) to the following areas: width and length of front bodice, width and length of back bodice, sleeve width, armscyes (the curve of the armholes) of sleeves, and bodice armscyes.

Templates

Plastic template material is available in quilt shops, art supply stores, office supply stores, and fabric shops. These are thin but durable plastic sheets that are specially constructed to be cut into templates, which will serve as your tracing guide when transferring the patchwork pattern to the fabric. Stiff cardboard also can be used for making templates. When using cardboard templates, check the edges of the template for wear after each use, and replace the template if it is worn. Worn or distorted templates will produce irregular-sized patchwork pieces, which will cause difficulty in the piecing of the blocks.

Tools

Scissors. A sharp pair of scissors, for fabric use only, is needed to cut the quilt-top fabrics. Paper scissors also should be kept handy to cut cardboard, paper, etc.
Ruler. A ruler is handy for straightening lines and for checking seam allowances. A transparent, gridded ruler is preferable for this purpose.
Charcoal Pencil. A charcoal pencil is handy for marking difficult-to-mark surfaces, such as plastic templates.
Washable Pens or #2 Soft Lead Pencil. A washable pen or #2 soft lead pencil is recommended for tracing designs and for transferring patchwork patterns.
Quilting Thimble. A quilting thimble, sometimes referred to as "finger saver," functions like a thimble. A quilting thimble is fitted to the hand opposite of the stitching finger's to protect the supporting finger while you are quilting. Quilting thimbles are available in most fabric stores. (Most quilters use thimbles on the sewing hand also, to push the needle through.)
Iron. An iron with a steam selection is recommended for a professional finish when pressing seams.

Needles. Regular hand-sewing needles of your choice are used for the piecing of the quilt top. However, short sharp needles, referred to as "betweens" (size #7 or #8 sharps), are recommended for quilting.

Sewing Machine. A sewing machine set for straight stitching at 8 to 10 stitches per inch (3.5 to 4 stitches per cm) is recommended for the construction of the garment and, if applicable, for assembling the patchwork pieces. Very small pieces may be more easily assembled with hand-stitching.

Quilting Hoop. A small quilting hoop is recommended to hold your work during the quilting process. It will smooth out the surface of the quilt while you stitch through the layers. A quilting hoop may be omitted for the smaller projects.

Sewing Gauge. A sewing gauge is a necessity in piecing the quilt top; it is used for checking the seam widths of the pieces. This handy gadget can also be used to check the markings of your seam allowances, which aids in precise piecing of the quilt top.

Pattern or Graph Paper. Gridded paper with boxes measuring 1″ on a side is handy for enlarging the apparel patterns in this book. You can also draw 1″ boxes on standard graph paper that is ruled with ¼″ boxes, which is available in many school-supply stores. Another possibility is to create your own graph paper by gridding the paper yourself. Large-sized illustration paper suitable for apparel patterns is available in art supply stores.

Colored Pencils or Crayons. These are helpful in planning your quilt-top designs and transferring them to your apparel patterns.

Material and Thread

Your choices of materials will determine the durability, care, and finished appearance of the garment you make. Materials for a quilt include quilt-top fabrics for the patchwork designs and background fabric, batting, backing fabric, and thread.

Quilt-Top Fabrics

I recommend 100% cotton and cotton-blend fabrics for quilting projects. Cotton blends should not have more than 50% synthetic fibres. Cotton and cotton blends can be ironed easily. However, this recommendation should not deter you from experimenting. Synthetics and other natural fabrics in addition to cotton can become wonderful creations at the hands of an innovator.

When selecting quilt-top fabrics, limit the fabrics used in a project to one kind of fibre (for example, only cotton or only synthetic fabrics with similar fibre classifications). When choosing synthetics, use woven types only. Knitted synthetic fabrics are not suitable for quilting. Be sure to preshrink all fabrics (see "Fabric Preparation" in Chapter 3).

Batting

Prebonded polyester batting, sold by the yard, is recommended for wearable quilts. Polyester batting is washable, lightweight, warm, and durable. There will be even distribution of the prebonded polyester type of batting, which is desirable in making a wearable quilt, since it will be hung on the body. Prebonded batting is available in several weights and lofts. For projects in which small areas of appliqué are stuffed, you will need loose polyester batting.

Backing Material

For light-colored projects, unbleached or bleached cotton that is of comparable weight to the quilt-top fabrics is recommended as backing. For dark-colored projects, choose backing material in dark colors. Keep in mind that slight color bleeding will be less noticeable on dark surfaces and more apparent on light surfaces.

Thread

Two types of thread are used in a quilting project: sewing thread and quilting thread.

Sewing Thread. Sewing thread of cotton-covered polyester, also known as "all-purpose thread," is recommended for the piecing of cotton and cotton-blend materials, because of its durability. For 100% cotton fabrics, use 100% cotton mercerized thread. If synthetic fabrics are chosen, all-purpose thread of cotton-covered polyester, or thread of the same fibre classification as the fabric being sewn, is recommended.

Quilting Thread. Quilting thread is thicker than sewing thread. Quilting thread of cotton-covered polyester is now available in a wide range of colors in most fabric stores. The tensile strength (breaking strength) of cotton-covered polyester quilting thread is an important element in the making of wearable quilts.

3

The Quilting Process

Estimating Yardage Requirements

Yardage (fabric) requirements can be estimated without extensive or complex mathematical calculations. One method is to calculate yardage for quilt-top assembly by the "block system." The block system means that each apparel pattern piece to be quilted is first marked off into blocks of the pattern unit (for example, the Bow-Tie Block). From the block count, the amount of fabric needed for each color is calculated. The block-system method of calculating yardage is described below.

Step 1. Determine the Number of Blocks You Need. Make a template of the patchwork pattern block, without adding seam allowances to it. Draw the outline of the block directly onto your enlarged and adjusted apparel pattern pieces. (See Chapter 4 for details of enlarging and adjusting patterns.) You can use the sketches of the projects in the book to guide your positioning of the template on the pattern pieces. The blocks must cover each apparel pattern piece that is to be patchworked, including the ⅝″ seam allowances of the pattern pieces (see Figure 1). With colored markers, crayons, or pencils, fill in blocks drawn on your apparel patterns with the design motif. Then count the number of blocks needed for the total pattern. From this you can derive the total number of each piece needed. Calculate the total number of blue triangles, for example, by multiplying the number of blue triangles in one block by the total number of blocks drawn on your pattern. Remember to include parts of blocks also. Your colored sketch will also give you some idea of how the design will look on the finished garment. You may want to modify it if it isn't pleasing to you. For symmetrical pattern parts (e.g., right front bodice and left front bodice) you probably will want to lay out the blocks in a symmetrical manner, so that the same pattern element is at the same height and distance from the center body line on both parts.

Step 2. Estimate the Yardage Needed for Each Color Group. Trace out the quilt-top pattern templates onto cardboard or plastic and cut them out.

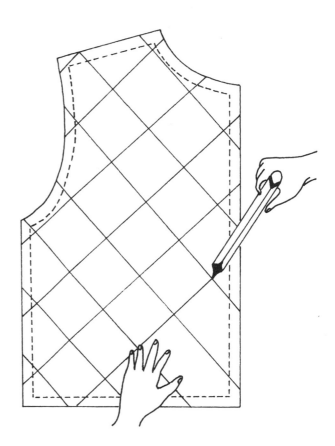

1. Determining the number of quilt-top pattern blocks needed for half a vest front. After enlarging and adjusting the pattern and adding seam allowances of ⅝″ (1.6 cm), use a full-sized pattern block as a template to trace blocks directly onto your paper pattern piece, covering the entire surface, including the apparel pattern's seam allowances. Take care in positioning the blocks so that both vest fronts are symmetrical and the design is well laid out. Then count the number of blocks needed, including partial blocks. Blocks are traced without seam allowances being added to them.

From your calculations in Step 1, you know how many of each template and each color of material you will need. Take a large sheet of paper for each color of material you will be using. Trace the calculated number of each template onto your paper for that color of material, adding seam allowances of ¼″ (.6 cm) around the drawing of each template as you go. For example, take one paper for navy blue if you are using navy blue in your design. Let's assume you have estimated in Step 1 you will need 10 navy-blue triangles and 10 navy-blue squares. Using your triangle and square templates, trace 10 triangles and 10 squares onto your paper that represents the navy-blue material, leaving ¼″ seam allowances around each piece you trace. Then measure the total of navy blue yardage you will need with a ruler (see Figure 2). Repeat this process with the appropriate templates for any other colors of material you will need in piecing the project.

Keep in mind that fabrics commonly sold in stores are 45″ to 46″ in width. A yardage conversion chart and a linear measure chart are included here to help you estimate how much fabric you need to buy in various fabric widths (see tables 2 and 3).

Yardage Conversion Tables

The accompanying yardage conversion tables are helpful for converting measurements from inches to yards, as well as for converting yardage estimates from a given yardage calculation in a pattern to an estimate for the fabrics you may have available.

The actual quilt-top preparation process involves: (1) fabric preparation; (2) tracing and cutting the quilt-top pattern; (3) piecing the quilt-top; (4) ironing the quilt-top; (5) basting the quilt-top, batting, and backing together; (6) marking the quilting stitches; and (7) joining the layers together by quilting.

Fabric Preparation

Always preshrink washable fabrics. The shape of a garment made with unshrunk fabric will be distorted with its first washing. If swatches of material are too small to be preshrunk, the garment they are made from should be dry-cleaned, rather than washed, to prevent shrinkage.

TABLE 2. YARDAGE CONVERSION CHART: EQUIVALENT AVAILABLE FABRIC AREAS FOR VARIOUS FABRIC WIDTHS

Fabric Width:	35″–35″	44″–46″	50″	52″–54″	58″–60″
Yardage Equivalents					
	1¾	1⅜	1¼	1⅛	1
	2	1⅝	1½	1⅜	1¼
	2¼	1¾	1⅝	1½	1⅜
	2½	2⅛	1¾	1¾	1⅝
	2⅞	2¼	2	1⅞	1¾
	3⅛	2½	2¼	2	1⅞
	3⅜	2¾	2⅜	2¼	2
	3¾	2⅞	2⅝	2⅜	2¼
	4¼	3⅛	2¾	2⅝	2⅜
	4½	3⅜	3	2¾	2⅝
	4¾	3⅝	3¼	2⅞	2¾
	5	3⅞	3⅜	3⅛	2⅞

Note: Reading across will give you equivalent areas of available fabric in various fabric widths. For example: 1¾ yards (63″) of 35″ wide material will give you 2268 in² of material; 1⅜ yards (49.6 in) of 45″ wide material will give you 2232 in² of material; 1¼ yards (44″) of 50″ wide material will give you 2200 in² of material; 1⅛ yards (40.5″) of 54″ wide material will give you 2187 in² of material; and 1 yard (36″) of 60″ wide material will give you 2160 in² of material; all the areas on one line across are approximately equal.

TABLE 3. CONVERSION OF INCHES TO YARDS (LINEAR MEASURE)	
Inches	Yards
36	1
27	¾
22.5	⅝
18	½
13.5	⅜
12	⅓
9	¼
4.5	⅛

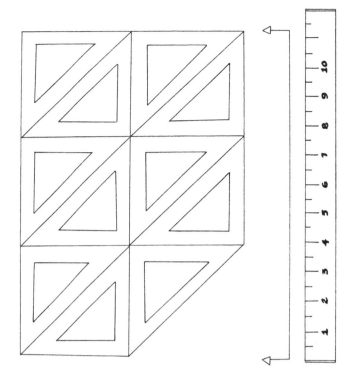

To preshrink fabrics, soak them overnight in cool water and liquid dish-washing soap. If dye is apparent in the water, rinse the fabric until the water remains clear and repeat the soaking process. If the dye still bleeds into the water, identify the fabric that is bleeding by placing the rinsed, wet material pieces on a light fabric surface of some old material you don't mind staining. The color bleeder will leave dye on the light-colored fabric. Remove the pieces that bleed from your project materials and don't use them.

Tracing and Cutting the Quilt-Top Pattern

Transferring the quilt-top pattern from template to fabric is a simple procedure. Use a soft, #2 graphite pencil or a washable pen for tracing. The template you use for tracing should *not* include seam allowances. Add seam allowance of ¼″ (.6 cm) around each piece after tracing it. (See the section above, "Estimating Yardage Requirements," to determine how many pieces to trace.) A sewing gauge or transparent ruler will be handy in marking and checking the seam allowances. Following the procedure described above will enable precision piecing of the quilt-top. Use sharp fabric scissors to cut the fabric pieces for the quilt-top. Cut one piece at a time to ensure uniformity of size of the quilt-top pieces.

Piecing the Quilt-Top

The quilt-top may be pieced by hand or by machine. Patterns with very small pieces and patterns containing curved seams may require hand-piecing, as small pieces are difficult to work with in the sewing machine. Pieced patchwork and appliqué are the two methods used in piecing of the quilt-tops given in this book.

2. Estimating the yardage needed for each color. Working with one color of fabric at a time, take a large piece of paper and the totals for each patchwork piece needed that you calculated earlier. On the paper, trace around the first template to be sewn in that color, adding ¼″ (.6 cm) seam allowances around it after it is traced. Continue tracing the first template until you have drawn enough pieces for your pattern in that color and template. Then take any other templates that will be used on the same color fabric and repeat the process on the same paper. Measure the total area your traced templates take up. This will give you an estimate of the amount of material of that color you will need.

Pieced Patchwork

Pieced patchwork for many projects in this book use strip-piecing or Seminole patchwork. In strip-piecing, fabric pieces are sewn into rows that later are joined together to form a quilt block or the entire quilt-top. (See Figure 3 for details.) Seminole patchwork may be done by joining two pieces by hand (Figure 4). Another method of doing Seminole patchwork is to use the strip-piecing method. Units are pieced in strips, cut, and then resewn to form bands (Figures 5 and 6). Bands are then pieced to form the quilt-top. The Seminole patchwork method offers limitless possibilities for clothing (see Figure 7).

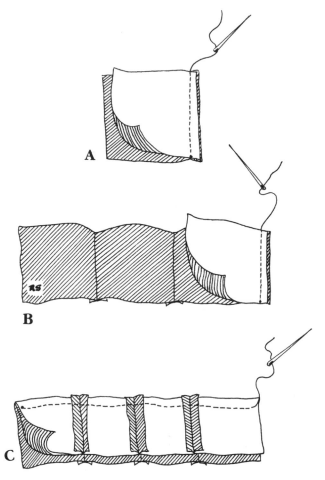

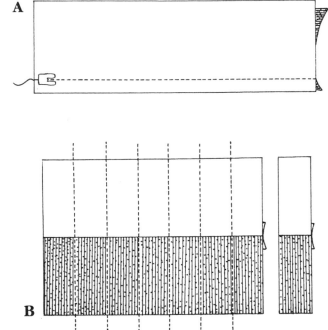

3. Piecing patchwork.   A: piecing two square patches.   B: a row of patches.   C: joining two rows. The same procedure could be done by machine.

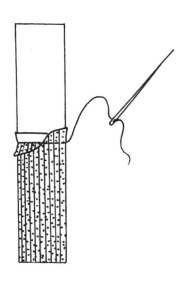

5. Seminole patchwork.   A: two large pieces of fabric are pieced by machine. Sew one dark strip and one light strip to make a large band.   B. Press the seams open, then measure and mark slices across the band of the desired width. Remember to include seam allowances in your calculations. Cut slices as indicated by the dotted lines.

4. Piecing two patches for Seminole patchwork by the hand method.

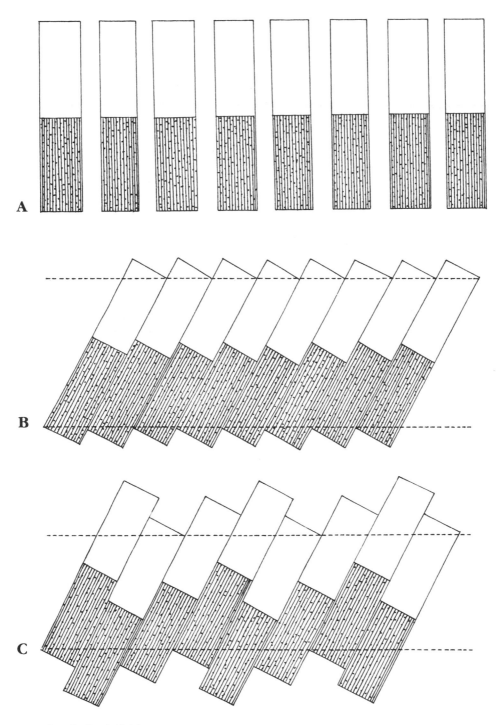

6. A: the individual two-patch units for Seminole patchwork.   B and   C: strips can be sewn together and recut (dotted lines) to achieve different effects.

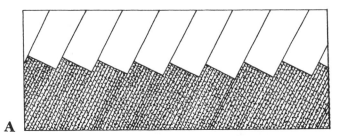

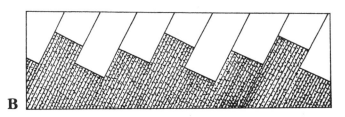

A

B

7A and B: Finished Seminole bands made from cutting as shown in 6B and 6C.

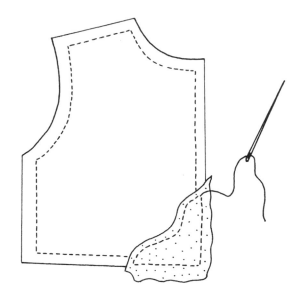

8. Crazy quilt, Step 1. Stitch one patch in a corner of the backing to begin hand-piecing the quilt-top.

Appliqué

Appliqué is a piecing method that involves putting a cut-out piece of material onto a larger piece of fabric and sewing it in place. (The word *appliqué* means "applied" or "put on" in French.) Appliqué is often used to make pictorial motifs. In hand appliqué the whipstitch or buttonhole stitch is used to secure the appliquéd pieces. (See Chapter 5, Figure 13, for illustrations of stitches.) We will discuss three appliqué techniques: crazy-quilt piecing, direct appliqué, and reverse appliqué.

Crazy-Quilt Piecing

Piecing of the quilt-top in crazy-quilt piecing can be done on either a fabric backing or on a paper backing, and by hand or by machine. The fabric backing will remain in place after you complete the piecing. To hand-appliqué the crazy-quilt pieces onto paper, start in one corner, as shown in Figure 8. Succeeding pieces are attached to each other (Figure 9), with seam allowances turned under. When all patches are joined, carefully remove the paper from the material. To hand-appliqué onto cloth, start in one corner of the pattern piece as shown in Figure 8 and appliqué a piece onto the cloth background, without turning its seam allowances under. Place the next patchwork piece so that its side touches the previous piece after its seam

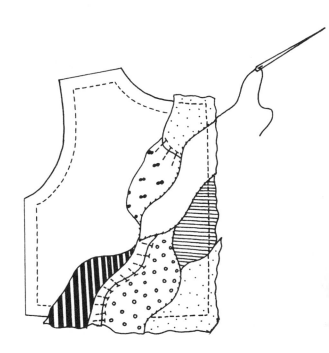

9. Crazy quilt, Step 2. Overlap the patches and secure the raw edges by turning them under. Whipstitch each succeeding patch to the previous patches.

allowance of ¼″ (.6 cm) is turned under (see Figure 9). Each succeeding piece is added in the same way, until the whole area to be crazy-quilted is filled, including the seam allowances of the pattern piece.

To do machine crazy-quilting, start in the middle of your pattern piece, rather than at the corner. Work out towards the edges, attaching the pieces with a zigzag or satin stitch, or some other decorative stitch. Turn under seam allowances as you go.

Direct Appliqué

Direct appliqué involves the application of a fabric patch or patches directly onto the background fabric. The appliquéd patches may be any shape you want, including flowers, hearts, and leaves. Direct appliqué may be done by hand or by machine.

Direct Appliqué by Hand. To do direct appliqué by hand:

1. Make a drawing of the shape you wish to appliqué. Trace it onto a template material such as plastic or cardboard and cut out the template.

2. Choose the fabric for the appliquéd piece. We will call this Fabric A.

3. Trace the template shape onto Fabric A (see Figure 10A).

4. Draw a ¼″ (.6 cm) seam allowance around the template after tracing it (see Figure 10B).

5. Cut out the figure to be appliquéd on the cutting line.

6. Cut notches in the seam allowance of the curved areas to facilitate folding of the seam allowance (see Figure 10C).

7. Turn under the seam allowances and baste them in place with large running stitches (Figure 10D).

8. Pin the pieces to be appliquéd in place on the background and whipstitch them in place (see Figures 10E and 11A).

9. Optional: The pieces may be appliquéd in place by using buttonhole stitching for decorative as well as for functional purposes (see Figure 11B).

Direct Appliqué by Machine. If machine appliqué is chosen, first consult the manual of your sewing machine to see if there are any special instructions for machine appliqué. Then:

1. Trace the designs to be appliquéd onto a rectangular piece of fabric that is larger than the

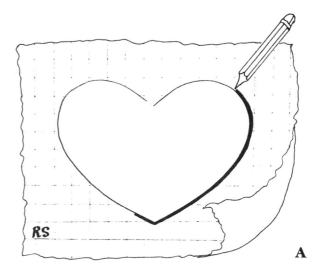

A

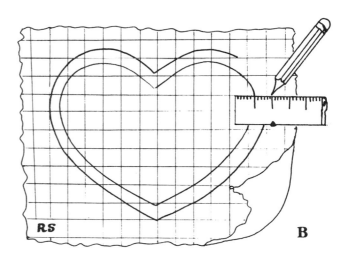

B

C

10. Direct appliqué, hand method.   A: trace the shape of the template on the material to be appliquéd.   B: trace a ¼″ (.6 cm) seam allowance around the shape and cut out the shape around the outside line.   C: Cut notches in the seam allowance of curved areas to facilitate folding.

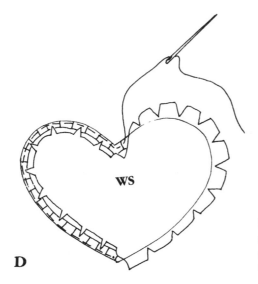

Direct appliqué, hand method, continued.   D: Sew down seam allowances on wrong side of appliqué with a running stitch close to the edge.   E: Pin and sew the appliqués on the backing material where desired.

D

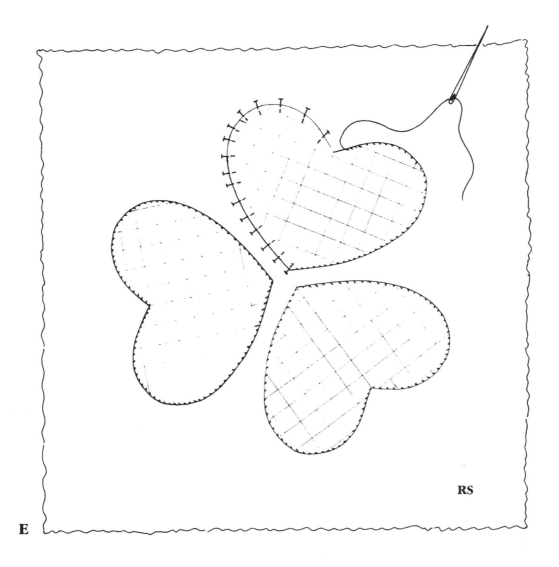

E

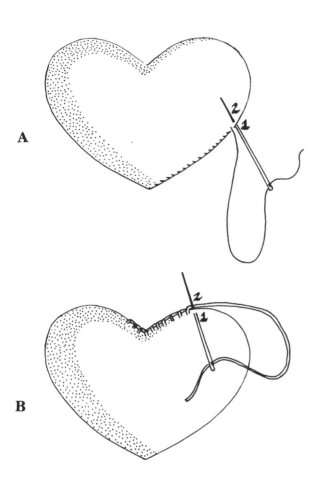

A

B

11.   A: Hand appliqué using whipstitching.
B: Hand appliqué using buttonhole stitching.

appliqué template in all directions by at least 1″. Do not cut out the shapes.

2. Tape the appliqué fabric onto the background material, carefully positioning the design where you want it to go.

3. Using a straight stitch, sew around the shape of the design ⅛″ (.3 cm) in from the outline, to anchor the material in place.

4. Trim away the excess material around the outline of the appliquéd shape.

5. Set your sewing machine for satin-stitch embroidery, insert an appropriate color for the embroidery, and satin-stitch all around the shape to be appliquéd, catching all the unfinished ends.

Reverse Appliqué

Reverse appliqué involves layering and cutting of quilt-top fabrics to expose the colors of the underlayers. The pattern is highlighted by the colors of the channels formed by this method (see Figure 12). It is best done by hand. Whipstitching and buttonhole stitching may be used to secure the cut edges if you work by hand.

Ironing

You may be familiar with the ironing method used for quilt-tops of bed quilts, in which seam allowances are pressed to one side. For wearable quilts, iron all the seams open after the quilt-top is pieced (see Figure 13). Ironing the seams open will give the quilt a smooth, even surface, and will distribute the areas of bulk and wear evenly throughout the garment. The quilt-top of a crazy quilt should be pressed flat before it is quilted.

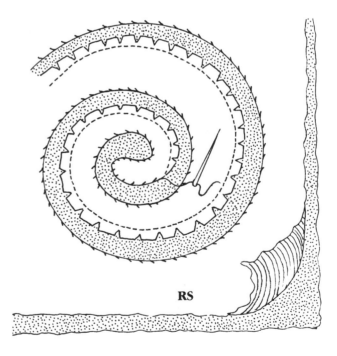

RS

12. Reverse appliqué. On the top material (white) a design is traced and cut, with extra fabric left for seam allowances. The seam allowances (notched areas) get turned under when the top material is stitched onto the background (grey areas).

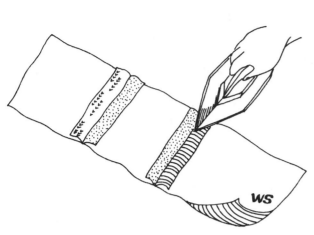

13. Ironing the seam allowances open.

Basting

Basting is needed to hold the quilt-top, batting, and backing together during the quilting process. When you baste the layers of the quilt, always begin from the central point of the piece you are quilting. Basting from the center will ensure a smooth, even surface on the finished quilt (see Figures 14 and 15).

14. Baste from the center of each piece to ensure a smooth surface.

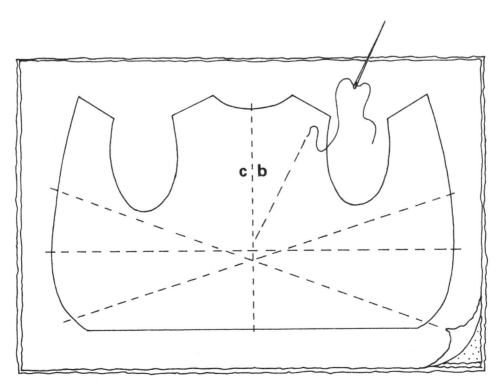

15. Basting a one-piece garment. Baste from the center back (cb) of the garment.

Marking the Quilting Stitches

It is extremely important to avoid having any permanent marks on the finished quilt-top. For this reason, use a soft, #2 graphite pencil or a washable pen in marking the quilting lines on your project. They will wash off easily when you are done. If you choose an intricate quilting pattern, work the design out on paper before transferring it to the fabric. You can then perforate the paper by pricking the quilting lines with a pin or large needle and mark through the pinholes with a pencil or washable pen. For straight lines, masking tape can be used as a guideline for the quilting stitches. Place the tape directly on the fabric where you want a line to be. Use the side of the tape as a guideline for sewing your row of quilting stitches. Remove and reposition the tape as necessary for the next line.

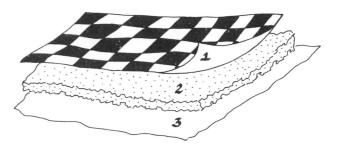

16. Layers of a quilt: 1, quilt-top; 2, batting; 3, backing.

Quilting the Layers

A quilt is often described as a "fabric sandwich." It derives its nickname from the layered materials that are stitched together to form a quilt (see Figure 16). We will mainly use two techniques in quilting: English or wadded quilting and trapunto (stuffed quilting).

English or Wadded Quilting

Wadded quilting indicates three-layered quilts, made of the quilt-top, batting (wadding), and backing fabric. In wadded quilting, a running stitch is used to hold the layers together. From 5 to 12 stitches per inch (3 to 5 per cm) are desirable, depending on the thickness of the quilting thread, the weight of the quilt-top fabrics, and the loft of the batting.

You may want to hold your work in an embroidery hoop to keep it from moving around while you quilt and to ensure a smooth surface. A quilting hoop is portable and has great mobility. It is especially suitable for small projects like wearable quilts. Be sure to baste all the layers together before placing the piece to be quilted in the quilting hoop.

To start quilting, tie a single knot in your quilting thread, insert the needle through the top and into the batting, and pull the knot through into the batting (Figure 17A) to hide it. To end a thread, tie a single knot and pull the needle and knot through to the batting before cutting the thread (see Figure 17B). Check the stitching periodically to be sure that all layers are being stitched securely. To avoid many endings and beginnings of threads, pass the needle under the top layer of fabric and come up in an adjacent area when you finish quilting one area (Figure 18).

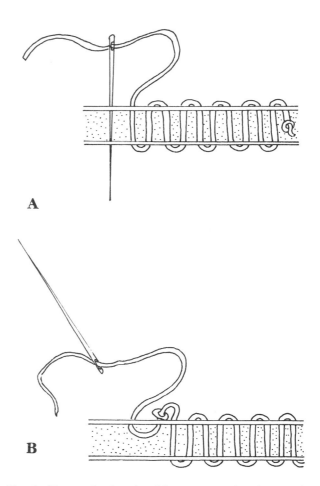

17. A: To start the hand-quilting process, tie a knot and pull it through to the batting to hide it.   B: To cut off or end the thread, tie a single knot and pull it through to the batting before cutting it.

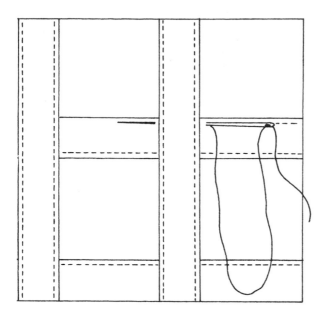

18. Continuous hand-quilting. Thread can be used without ending it by taking the needle under the top layer of fabric and quilting adjacent areas.

Common Quilting Stitches

Quilt stitching can enhance the quilt, in addition to securing its layers. Some common quilt stitches are the outline, figurative, scallop, vertical, horizontal, and diagonal stitches (see Figure 19).

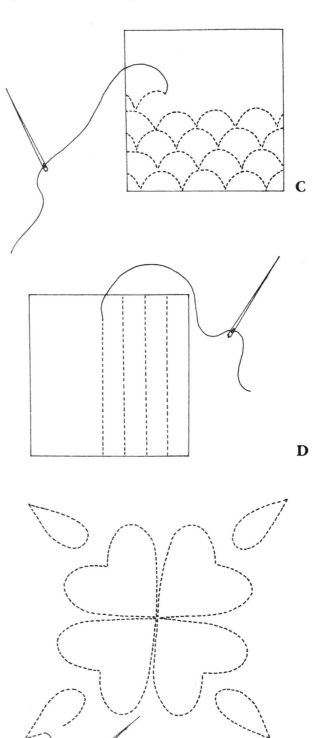

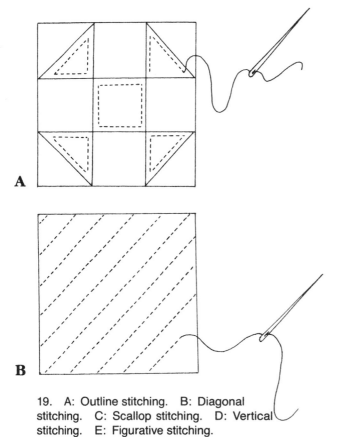

19. A: Outline stitching. B: Diagonal stitching. C: Scallop stitching. D: Vertical stitching. E: Figurative stitching.

Trapunto (Stuffed Quilting)

Trapunto, also known as stuffed quilting, uses raised designs to enhance the surface of the quilt. The design is raised by stuffing selected spaces between the front and back of the quilt with some sort of filling—for example, batting. Unlike wadded quilting, there is no layer of batting spread overall between the front and back of the quilt in trapunto. To effectively raise the design on the front of the quilt, use a crisp backing material, which will offer resistance and force the stuffing towards the softer layer (namely, the front of the quilt).

To do trapunto, outline the design you wish to have filled through the two layers of the quilt, using either matching or contrasting quilting thread and running stitches (Figure 20A). Then turn the quilt over so the backing faces up. Slash an opening in the backing material only, in the center of the area to be stuffed with batting. Take care not to slash the front of the quilt. Then stuff loose batting in the area you wish to raise, adjust it as necessary, and sew up the slash with whipstitching (Figure 20B).

Trapunto also can be used to enhance collars, lapels, and cuffs. It is effective in highlighting figurative patchwork motifs, or as an overall pattern for a quilt.

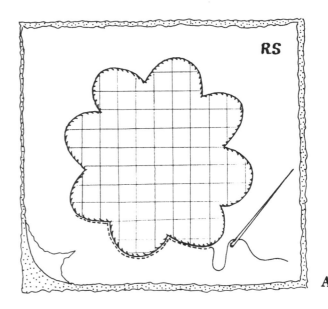

A

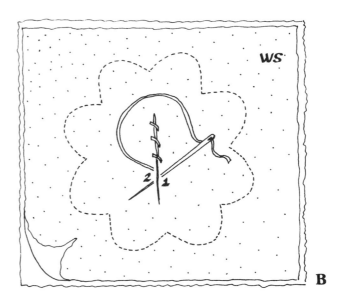

B

20. Trapunto (stuffed quilting) with batting insertion.
A: Running stitches outline the motif through the quilt-top and backing material.   B: Turn the quilt to the wrong side (w.s.), and make a slash through the backing material only, in the design area to be raised. Stuff loose batting in the area to be filled, adjusting it as necessary. Close the opening with whipstitching.

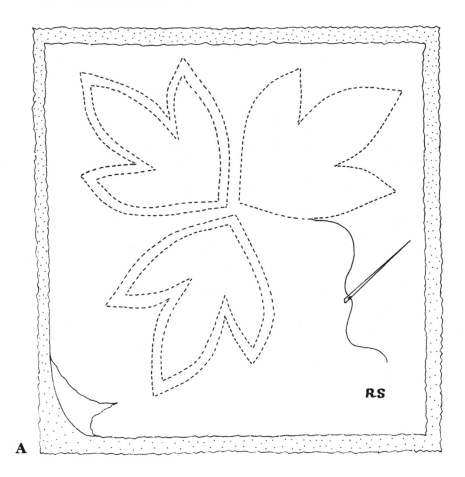

A

Italian Quilting

Italian quilting is another method of raising certain parts of a quilt that does not have a middle batting layer overall. Italian quilting uses channels of stitches sewn to accommodate yarn or cord. To insert yarn, sew a design with quilting thread that has two rows of running stitches of a distance apart suitable to be filled by yarn (see Figure 21A). Working from the back of the quilt, insert the yarn between the two layers of material and between the two rows of stitches. Choose a yarn that will not shrink when washed, or prewash it to be sure it won't shrink. Make yarn loops in the quilt back in the curved areas, to add the slack needed to keep the quilt from puckering. End off the yarn on the back layer of the quilt (Figure 21B).

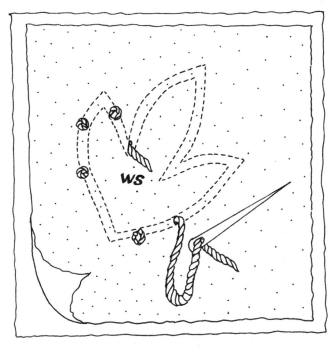

B

21. Italian quilting (yarn insertion).   A: Two lines of running stitches outline the motif through the quilt-top and backing material.   B: From the wrong side of the quilt, insert the yarn in the space between the running stitches. Be sure to form loops for slack in curved areas to keep them from puckering.

4

Enlarging and Adjusting an Apparel Pattern's Size

Enlarging Apparel Patterns

The apparel patterns in this book are drawn on a scale of one box = 1 in.^{2} (boxes are 2.5 cm on a side). To enlarge the patterns, draw a grid of lines 1″ (2.5 cm) apart on some kind of large, sturdy paper. If you have access to graph paper, you can use it. Label the lines on your small pattern and correspondingly on your large paper, as shown in Figure 1. With a pencil, transfer the main points from the pattern onto the grid of your large paper. The point at 1A on your small sketch should be drawn on your large paper at point 1A, for example. Then draw the connecting lines between your marks on the enlarged grid, using the small pattern as a guide.

Sizing of apparel patterns is based on the measurements given in Table 4.

Increasing the Size of a Pattern

After you have enlarged the pattern, check it against your own measurements. You may find it necessary to increase the size of some or all of the pattern parts, which requires only simple arithmetic and drafting abilities. To increase the pattern's size:

1. Draw intersecting lines on the pattern section to be increased, as shown in figures 2 and 3.

2. Calculate the amount of increase needed. For example, if you need to add 1″ (2.5 cm) to the front bodice width and ½″ (1.3 cm) to the front bodice length, you would want to distribute this amount equally in the center section of both bodice front pieces, indicated by the intersecting vertical lines of Figure 2A. Thus you would need

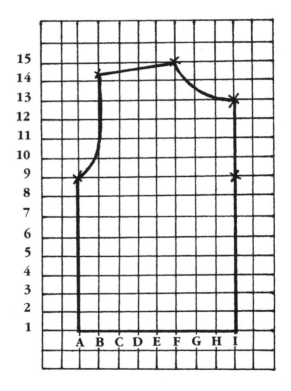

1. The patterns in this book are drawn on a scale of 1 box = 1 in.^{2} To enlarge the apparel patterns in this book, draw a full-scale grid of squares that are 1″ (2.5 cm) on a side. Label each line as shown here on both the small pattern and on your full-scale grid. Draw the corresponding points on the small pattern onto your large grid. Numbering the squares and lines will help in transferring the design. Connect the points to form an enlarged pattern.

TABLE 4.   SIZING USED IN APPAREL PATTERNS

Size	Bust	Waist	Hips
Small	32"–33" (81.3–83.8 cm)	25"–26" (63.5–66 cm)	34.5"–35.5" (87.7–90.2 cm)
Medium	36"–37" (91.4–94 cm)	28"–29" (71.1–73.7 cm)	38"–39" (96.5–99.1 cm)
Large	38"–39" (96.5–99.1 cm)	32"–33" (81.3–83.8 cm)	42"–43" (106.7–109.2 cm)
One size	Fits almost all size ranges. Additional ease may be desired for larger sizing.		

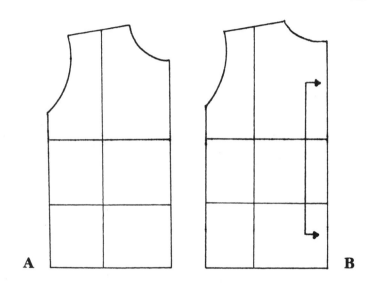

A   B

2. Intersecting lines for increasing or decreasing the front bodice (A) and the back bodice (B). Arrow indicates fold line.

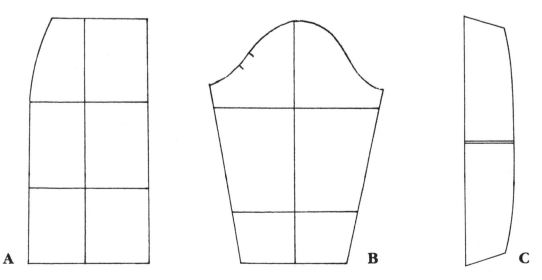

A   B   C

3. Intersecting lines for increasing or decreasing a skirt (A), a sleeve (B), or a collar (C).

to increase the width of each front section (if the front is divided in two) by ½″ (1.3 cm) for a total increase of 1″ (2.5 cm). To increase the length of the bodice a total of ½″, add ¼″ (.6 cm) at each of the two horizontal increase lines. Cut the pattern piece apart along the intersecting lines, and paste or tape it on a larger paper, adding the amount of increase needed between the intersecting lines.

Figure 4 shows what the bodice in Figure 2 would look like when cut apart and spread apart to increase the size. Figure 3 gives increase/decrease lines for skirt, collar, and sleeve patterns.

Making an Apparel Pattern Smaller

Making an apparel pattern smaller is similar to making it larger. The difference is that the pattern sections are overlapped to decrease their dimensions, instead of being spread apart (see Figure 5).

1. Draw the intersecting lines on the pattern to be decreased (see Figures 2 and 3).

2. Calculate the amount you need to lose by measuring yourself and comparing the pattern pieces with the dimensions you need. Remember to distribute the size loss between the two halves of the bodice if you are decreasing a bodice pattern in width, for example.

3. Cut the pattern apart on the intersecting lines, measure the amount you need to decrease on the pattern with a ruler, and overlap the pattern pieces the correct amount. Glue or tape the pieces in place to form the adjusted pattern.

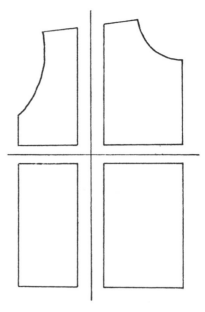

4. To increase the size of an apparel pattern, cut it along the intersecting lines and spread the sections apart by the amount needed. To increase width, spread the pattern at the vertical lines; to increase length, spread it at the horizontal lines.

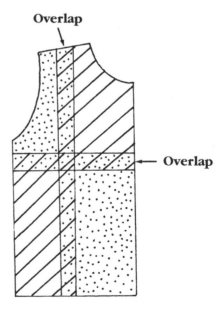

5. To decrease the size of an apparel pattern, cut it along the intersecting lines and overlap the sections by the amount of decrease needed. To decrease width, overlap on the vertical lines. To decrease length, overlap on the horizontal lines.

5

Finishing

"Finishing" is a term that describes the additional work done on a garment beyond its basic construction. Finishing includes embellishment as well as functional steps; for example, both embroidery and securing the raw edges of material to keep them from ravelling are part of finishing.

Making Bias Binding

Bias binding is available commercially in various widths and lengths. If you choose commercial bias binding, I recommend the kind with a finished width of ½" (1.3 cm) for the projects in this book. [Its unfolded width is 2" (5 cm).] However, to match the fabrics of your project, it is relatively simple to make your own bias binding, as described below:

1. Determine the length of bias tape you will need by measuring around the pattern where bias binding is needed.

2. Calculate the yardage by multiplying the length by the width of the unfolded bias binding, allowing some extra yardage. (Remember that it is cut across the fabric on a diagonal.)

3. Preshrink the fabric to be used for bias binding if the garment is to be washed.

4. Press the fabric to remove wrinkles.

5. Draw a square with edges parallel to the straight grain of your fabric, about ½" (1.3 cm) in from the edge. If your material has a selvage, this may be used as a guide to the straight grain (Figure 1).

6. Mark the cutting lines for the bias tape by drawing diagonally from one corner of the square to the opposite corner of the square.

7. Continue marking your cutting lines (Figure 2). For bias tape whose finished width is ½" wide (1.3 cm wide), the unfolded bias tape should measure 2" (5 cm). [The finished (folded) width of bias tape is ¼ of its unfolded width, for any size.]

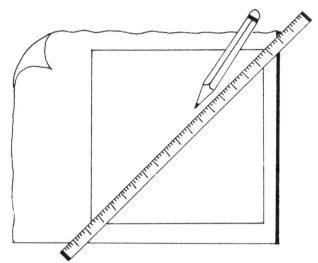

1. To make bias strips, first mark a large square along the straight grain of the fabric. Then mark a line on the diagonal of the square. The heavy line is the selvage.

2. Mark parallel lines the correct distance apart to make bias strips. The unfolded width of the strip is 4 times the final (folded) width.

8. Cut your bias strips as precisely as possible. The ends of each strip will taper diagonally. When piecing them into a long strip, match the edge with another strip, as shown in Figure 3. With right sides together, sew your bias strips together to create a long piece of bias binding. Press the seams open.

9. Trim off the protruding ends of the seams where the pieces join (Figure 4).

Applying Bias Binding

To finish the raw edges of a garment with bias binding:

1. With right sides of the fabrics facing, pin and baste the bias tape to the outside of the garment (Figure 5).

2. Sew the tape to the garment along the seam line. Machine stitch if possible as it is strongest.

3. Grade and notch the seam allowances for shaping (Figure 6).

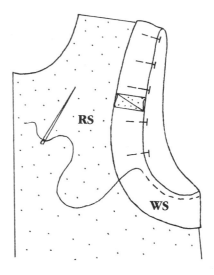

5. Bias binding pinned on the outside of a bodice section and sewn in place. Sewing can be done by hand or by machine.

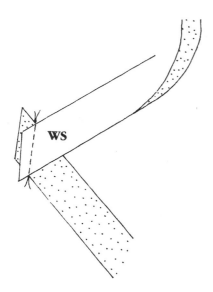

3. With right sides together, join two strips of bias tape.

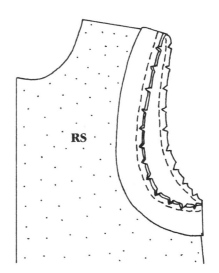

6. Grade and notch seam allowances of the bias binding and the armhole seam.

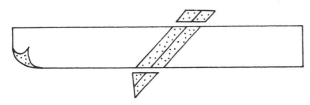

4. Trim off the excess fabric at the seam lines of the bias tape.

4. Turn the unattached edge of the bias tape to the wrong side of the garment, fold the raw edge under, and pin and press it in place. Secure the bias tape on the inside with whipstitching (Figure 7).

Roulou Loops

Roulou loops are used in place of buttonholes in bulky projects, or they may be added for decorative applications. To make roulou loops:

1. Cut bias strips 1″ (2.5 cm) wide and of correct length for the button that you have chosen for the project. This includes a seam allowance of ¼″ (.6 cm). Make certain that the loop has ample room to hold the button, to facilitate ease in fastening or unfastening the closure.

2. With right sides of material facing in, fold the strip lengthwise. Sew the side seam, closing one end, making the loop about ⅛″ wide (.3 cm); see Figure 8. Trim the sewn seam allowances to ⅛″ (.3 cm).

3. Turn the roulou loop inside out by pushing a crochet hook into the closed end of the loop (Figure 9).

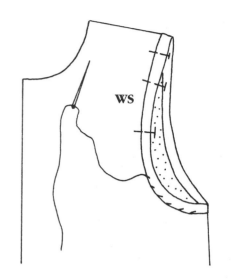

7. Turn the tape over to the wrong side of the fabric. Pin, press, and whipstitch the bias tape in place.

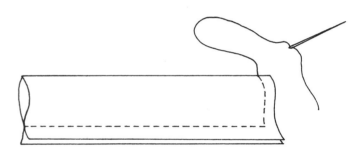

8. Sewing a roulou loop. Leave one short end open.

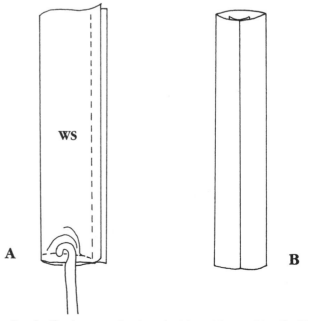

9. A: Turning a roulou loop inside out by pushing it with a crochet hook. B: The loop after being turned.

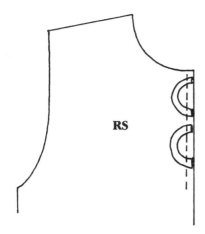

10. Baste roulou loops to the outside of the garment.

4. For a vest, baste the roulou loop to the outside of the garment with the rounded part away from the edge of the garment (see Figure 10).

5. With right sides of material together, sew bias tape to the raw edges of the garment (Figure 11).

6. Trim and notch seam allowances on curves and corners.

7. Turn the bias tape towards the wrong side of the garment, leaving ¼″ on the right side of the garment. Fold the raw edge of the bias tape under and whipstitch the bias tape to the inside of the garment. The finished loops will appear as in Figure 12.

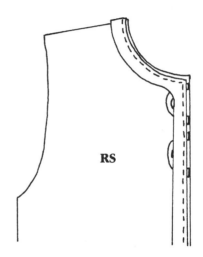

11. With right sides of material facing, sew bias tape over the roulou loops along the outside edge.

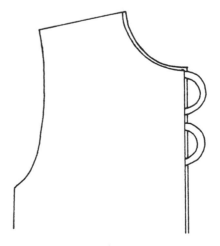

12. The finished roulou loops attached to the garment.

Machine Finishes

Zigzag stitching and overlock stitching are recommended for finishing the projects in this book. See the text of each project for further details.

Hand Finishes

Hand finishes used for the projects in this book include overcast stitching, buttonhole stitching, and enclosed seam binding (see figures 13A through 13D). Hand finishes offer flexibility to the seams, especially in stress areas such as the neckline and armholes.

Embroidery Stitches

The embroidery stitches that were used for the projects in the book include the running stitch, buttonhole stitch, and the featherstitch (see figures 13D through 13F).

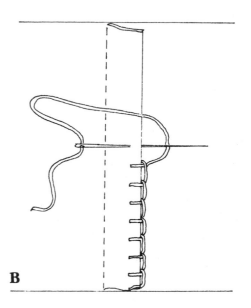

B

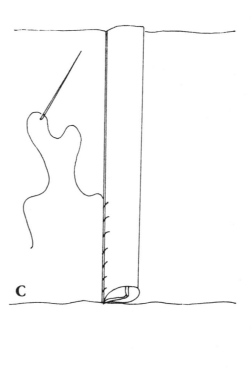

C

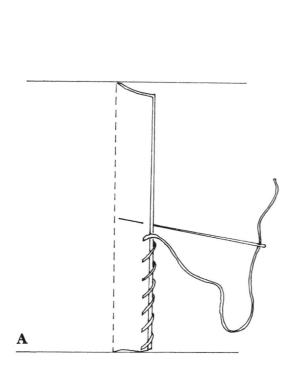

A

13. Various stitches (above and opposite page).   A: overcast or whipstitching on a seam.   B: buttonhole stitching on a seam.   C sewing enclosed seam binding with whipstitching.   D: The running stitch. E: The buttonhole stitch done as an embroidery stitch.   F: The featherstitch.

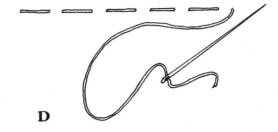

D

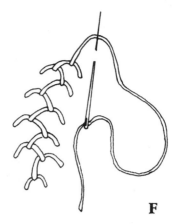

F

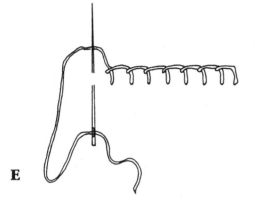

E

Meandering Vines Vest

1. Meandering Vines Vest, front and back views.

The graceful lines of meandering vines inspired the quilted vest shown in Figure 1 and color page A. To create the rhythmic formation of the vines, bias tape is appliquéd to the quilt-top (Figure 2). The folded width of the bias tape I used for the meandering vines was ¼″ (.6 cm). Its unfolded width was 1″, which included seam allowances. The width of the bias tape is up to you, however. Choose the size with which you are comfortable.

Materials

- Solid cotton fabric for the background of the quilt-top
- Fabric of similar color for the backing: 27″ (68.6 cm) of 45″ (114.3 cm) wide fabric for medium size
- Bias tape of a solid hue for finishing the project (edging armholes, neck, and bottom); the width of the solid-colored tape unfolded = 2″, folded width = ½″ (1.3 cm). For medium-sized pattern, about 3 yards (274 cm)
- Bias tape for vines, of a print or of a contrasting hue to the background fabric. I used tape that was ¼″ when folded (1″ unfolded). (The folded width is ¼ of the unfolded width.)
- Polyester batting: 27″ (68.6 cm) of 45″ (114.3 cm) wide batting for medium size
- Sewing thread of a matching hue to the background fabric
- Quilting thread of a matching hue to the background fabric
- Sewing thread of a matching hue to the appliquéd bias tape (vines)
- Basting thread
- 3 Shanked buttons
- 3 roulou loop closures (see Chapter 5 for roulou loops)
- Apparel Pattern #2, Asymmetrical Vest (page 117)

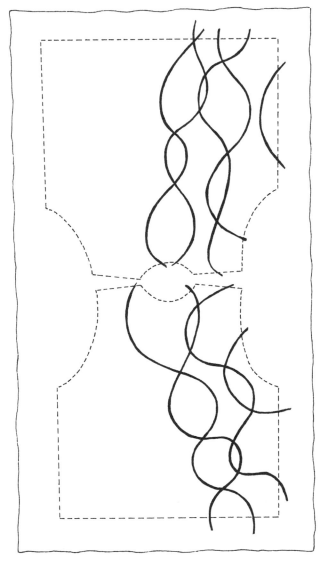

2. Diagram for bias tape layout.

Directions

1. Preshrink the background fabric, backing fabric, and bias tapes.

2. Enlarge and adjust Apparel Pattern #2 (see Chapter 4 for enlarging and adjusting instructions). Add ⅝″ (1.6 cm) seam allowances around all pattern pieces.

3. Iron the background fabric, backing, and bias tape to remove any wrinkles.

4. Cut rectangles of the background fabric large enough to fit the front and back bodice patterns (see Apparel Pattern #2, Figure 3). Do not cut out the pattern shapes yet from the fabric, however.

5. Trace the apparel patterns onto the background fabric.

6. Pin the bias tapes in the meandering vine design onto the outside of the background fabric (see Figure 2).

7. Appliqué the bias tapes in place with whipstitching (see Figure 3).

8. After the bias tapes are appliquéd, iron the quilt-top pieces to flatten the surface.

9. Cut the backing and batting rectangles about 1″ larger on each side than the background fabric rectangles for the front and back bodice pieces. Do not cut them to shape yet, however.

10. Baste together the quilt-top, batting, and backing rectangles for the front bodice. Repeat the process for the back bodice. Remember to baste away from the center of each bodice piece (see basting instructions in Chapter 3).

11. Quilt the front and back bodice pieces with diagonal lines of quilting stitches about ½″ (1.3 cm) apart. See the color illustration of the project for the quilting lines.

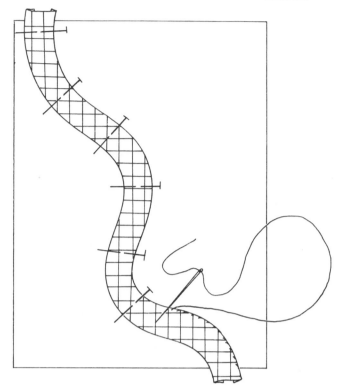

3. Whipstitching is used to attach the bias tapes by hand. Zigzag stitch by machine also could be used.

12. Remove the basting stitches after quilting.

13. Stay-stitch ¹⁄₁₆″ (.16 cm) outside of the seam lines of the vest around all the vest parts, using the widest zigzag stitch on your sewing machine. This step will prevent the quilting stitches from coming apart after you cut the bodice pieces to shape.

14. Cut out the bodice pieces along the cutting lines.

15. Construct the vest according to the directions in Apparel Pattern #2.

PROJECT 2
Strip-Quilt Vest

1. Strip-Quilt Vest, front and back views.

A vest made with strip-quilting, a simple method of piecing a quilt-top, is an excellent project for the novice quilter (see Figure 1 and color page B). The fabric strips that comprise the quilt-top can be pieced by hand or by machine. For added interest, plan the strips in varying widths, from ¾″ (.6 cm) to 2″ (5 cm). Each section of the apparel pattern (the right front bodice, the left front bodice, and the back bodice) is pieced and quilted separately.

Materials

- Cotton fabrics in light solid colors, or light-colored prints
- Cotton fabrics in dark solid colors, or dark-colored prints
- Polyester batting: 1 yard (91.4 cm) of 46″ (116.8 cm) wide batting for medium size
- Backing material: 1 yard (91.4 cm) of 46″ (116.8 cm) wide fabric for medium size
- Bias tape whose finished width is ½″ (1.3 cm); unfolded width is 4″ (10.2 cm): 3¼ yards (297 cm) for finishing. Add 27″ (68.6 cm) for ties
- Sewing thread, 1 spool of a dark color
- Quilting thread: 1 spool of a dark color; 1 spool of a light color
- Button (optional)
- Basting thread
- Apparel Pattern #1, Basic Vest (page 115)

Directions

1. Enlarge and adjust Apparel Pattern 1 (see Chapter 4 for instructions on enlarging and adjusting). Add ⅝″ (1.6 cm) seam allowances around paper pattern pieces on all sides. Measure the area of your pattern pieces to estimate how much fabric you will need for the backing. Measure around the edges of the vest to estimate how much bias binding you will need to make to finish the project.

2. Sketch the design on your paper patterns, using colored pencils or crayons.

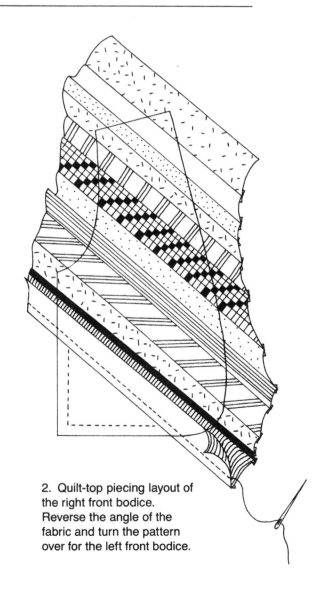

2. Quilt-top piecing layout of the right front bodice. Reverse the angle of the fabric and turn the pattern over for the left front bodice.

3. Preshrink the fabrics, the backing material, and the bias tape.

4. Iron the fabrics and the backing material to remove any wrinkles.

5. Cut strips of fabrics for the quilt-top of varying widths, based on your sketch, along the straight grain of the fabric, adding ¼″ (.6 cm) on each side around each strip on your sketch for seam allowances. Determine the length of strips needed by measuring diagonally across the front pieces of your apparel pattern (see Figure 2) and straight up and down across the back piece (see Figure 3). Cut the strips a few inches longer than your measurements; you can trim them later on.

6. Sew the strips together on their long sides, using a ¼″ (.6 cm) seam allowance. Keep adding strips until you create enough material in this manner to more than cover the area of the front bodice piece as shown in Figure 2. Repeat the process for the left front bodice piece. You probably will want the two sides to be symmetrical, so cut and piece the material strips together in the same order for the left front bodice as you did for the right (see Figure 1).

7. After piecing the strips, iron all the seams open.

8. The fabric strips for the front bodice are placed on the apparel pattern diagonally to emphasize the wearer's face (see Figure 2). Position the fabric strips symmetrically for both bodice fronts (see Figure 1). The fabric strips for the back bodice are positioned vertically.

9. Using tailor's chalk or dressmaker's carbon, trace the apparel pattern for the right front bodice onto the material you pieced for the right bodice. Set it aside. Repeat the process for the left front bodice.

10. Cut a rectangle of batting and of backing material for each piece of the apparel pattern, making it about 1″ (2.5 cm) larger on each side than the apparel pattern. Do not cut it to shape yet.

11. With a single thread, hand-baste the lining, batting, and the quilt-top together (see Figure 14 in Chapter 3 for reference). Remember to baste away from the center of each section to smooth out the fabric surface.

12. Following the seam lines of the patchwork quilt-top, quilt each bodice section with outline stitching (see page 34). Use light-colored thread for the light-colored strips and dark-colored thread for the dark-colored strips.

13. Remove the basting stitches after quilting.

14. Stay-stitch ¹⁄₁₆″ (.16 cm) outside of the seam lines of each vest piece, using the widest stitch of your sewing machine or hand stay-stitching. This will prevent the quilting stitches from coming out after you cut the bodice pieces to shape.

15. Cut out the three vest pieces along their cutting lines.

16. Construct the vest according to the directions in Apparel Pattern #1.

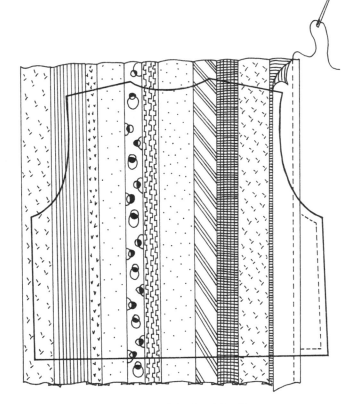

3. Quilt-top piecing layout of the back bodice.

Crazy-Quilt Kimono Jacket

1. Crazy-Quilt Kimono Jacket, front and back views.

Crazy quilting reached the height of its popularity during the Victorian era. Crazy quilts made of silks or velvets, embellished with intricate embroidery, graced many Victorian parlors and bedrooms. It had humble beginnings on the American frontier, when material was scarce and women saved even the tiniest scraps of fabrics for their quilts. Crazy quilting offers versatility in fabric selection and design (see color page C).

Materials

- Scraps of fabrics for crazy-quilt design
- Solid-colored fabric for cuffs, yoke, collar sash, hemband, and roulou loop
- Backing material: 4 yards (366 cm) of 46" (116.8 cm) wide fabric for all sizes
- Polyester batting: 4 yards (366 cm) of 46" (116.8 cm) wide batting for all sizes
- Quilting thread: 1 spool light and 1 spool dark
- Sewing thread: 1 spool light and 1 spool dark
- Basting thread
- Bias cording (optional)
- Button for holding jacket closed (optional)
- Embroidery floss (assorted colors)
- Apparel Pattern 3: Kimono Jacket (page 119)

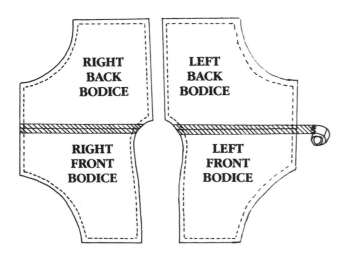

2. Tape the paper bodice pattern sections together at the shoulder seams.

Directions

The Kimono Jacket pattern (Apparel Pattern 3) has 8 pattern pieces: the right front bodice, the right back bodice, the right front yoke, the back yoke, the cuff, the back hemband, the front hemband, and the collar sash.

1. Enlarge and adjust the Kimono Jacket pattern, Apparel Pattern #3. (See Chapter 4 for enlarging and adjusting instructions.)

2. Take the enlarged and adjusted bodice apparel patterns. (The bodice pattern includes the sleeve.) Join the right front bodice and right back bodice patterns at the shoulder seams with adhesive tape (Figure 2). Reverse the right bodice patterns to make the left front bodice and left back bodice, and join them to form the left side of the jacket. Add ⅝" (1.6 cm) seam allowance around all the edges of the right and left bodice pattern papers (except the fold line). Make a second (duplicate) set of pattern pieces for the bodice units. One set will be used for appliquéing on the quilt-top. The second set will be used for tracing and shaping the quilt-top. Measure your pattern pieces to estimate how much fabric you will need for the backing, binding, and quilt-top scraps.

3. Preshrink all fabrics, including the backing material and the scrap fabrics.

4. Press all fabrics to remove wrinkles and set them aside.

5. Using the color photo in the photo section and the sketch (Figure 1) as guides, plan the crazy-quilt design you would like and draw it on one set of your bodice pattern pieces, using crayons or colored pencils. Following your sketch,

appliqué the scrap fabrics directly onto the paper patterns of your bodice. See Figure 3, as well as the appliqué instructions in Chapter 3, for guidance. Be sure to extend the crazy-quilt pieces to the edge of each pattern piece, including the pattern's seam allowances.

6. Iron the surface of the bodice sections after the appliqué process is completed.

7. Carefully peel the paper pattern off the back of each panel. It should peel off easily since perforations have been formed from the needle-holes you made as you pieced the quilt-top.

8. Lay out and trace the second copies of the left and right bodice patterns (which you made in Step 2) onto the quilt-top.

9. Set your sewing machine to its largest stitch and stay-stitch $\frac{1}{16}''$ (.16 cm) outside of the seam lines on each bodice piece. This will prevent the quilting stitches from coming apart after you cut the pieces to shape.

10. Cut out each bodice panel from the pieced fabric.

11. With right sides together, join the halves of the jacket bodice by sewing up the center back seam (Figure 4). Iron the seam open.

12. Take the enlarged and adjusted yoke patterns from Apparel Pattern #3 for the front and back yoke. Cut one back yoke pattern on folded paper and two front yoke patterns on paper. Add $\frac{5}{8}''$ (1.6 cm) seam allowances around each. Cut out the pattern pieces from solid-colored fabric. In our model, the yoke is dark blue (see color photo) as are the hembands, and cuffs, and collar sash.

13. With the right sides of the material together, sew the back yoke to the corresponding front yoke pieces (see Figure 5). Press the seams open.

14. With the right sides of the material together, sew the yokes to the bodice (see Figure 6). Notch the curved areas of the seams after sewing them, to keep the surface smooth. Press seams open. The back yoke and front yoke areas will be quilted along with the bodice of the jacket.

15. Cut a backing rectangle and a batting rectangle about 1″ (2.5 cm) larger on each side than the pieced bodice plus yoke (see Figure 7).

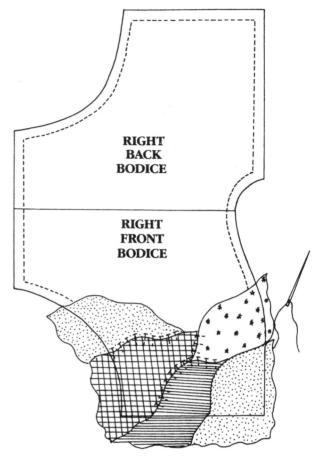

3. The crazy-quilt appliqué process requires the overlapping of pieces. The seam allowances are turned under and sewn to the previously applied pieces with whipstitching (if you quilt by hand) or by zigzag stitch if you machine-stitch.

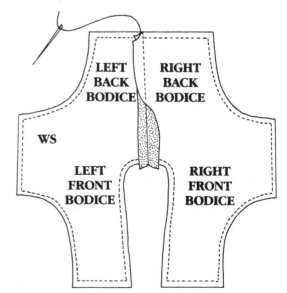

4. Sewing the bodice panels together at the center seam with right sides of material facing.

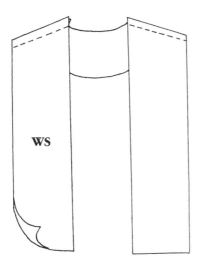

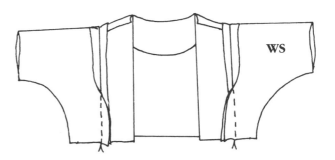

5. Sewing the front yokes to the back yoke, with right sides of material facing.

6. Sewing the yokes to the right and left bodice, with right sides of material facing.

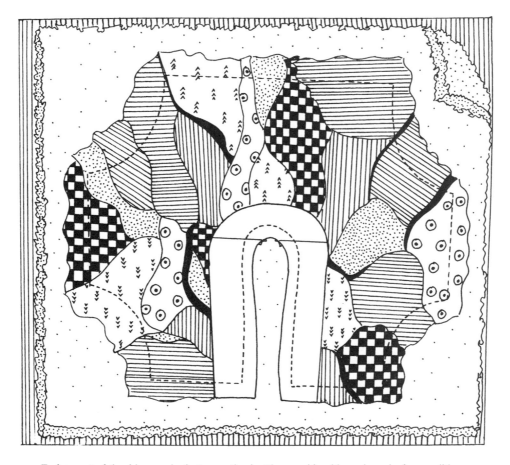

7. Layout of the kimono jacket over the batting and backing, done before quilting.

16. Baste the quilt-top, batting, and binding layers together (see basting instructions in Chapter 3).

17. Quilt the layers with a variety of quilting stitches, for surface interest. Some suggestions are shown in Figure 8.

18. Remove the basting stitches after quilting.

19. Apply embroidery as desired. Featherstitch embroidery is recommended for this project. (See color photo and embroidery stitches in Chapter 5.)

20. With right sides of bodice panels facing each other, seam the left bodice front to the left bodice back under the arm. Seam the right bodice front to the right bodice back under the arm also.

21. Take the enlarged and adjusted apparel patterns of the cuffs, collar, sash, and hemband that you made from Apparel Pattern 3. Add ⅝" (1.6 cm) seam allowance around the pattern pieces, except on the sides that represent fold lines. Check the sizes of each piece against the already constructed parts of the garment and adjust the patterns as needed. Cut out the correct number of each piece, as indicated on the patterns, from your solid-colored material.

22. Form the cuffs, the collar sash, and the hemband of the jacket as described in Apparel Pattern 3, steps 5 through 11. If you wish, quilt them after they are attached to the jacket, as shown in Figure 8.

23. Attach a button to the left front collar sash. Make and attach a roulou loop in the right front sash (see Chapter 5 for roulou loop instructions).

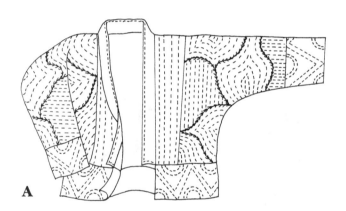 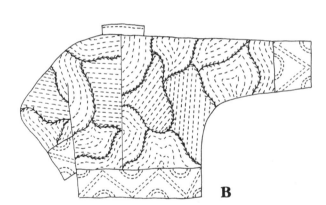

8. Suggested quilting patterns. A: Front view of the jacket. B: back view of the jacket.

Rose Medallion Vest

1. The Rose Medallion Vest, front and back views.

Country floral motifs are classic favorites in clothing. The Rose Medallion

Vest (Figure 1 and color page E) echoes the concept of delicate floral design.

Scraps of floral prints and solid fabrics are suitable for this project. See the

color photo of the project for one possible color combination.

Materials

- Solid red or pink cotton fabric for the rose and optional side bands
- Solid dark green cotton for the leaves
- Scraps of cotton prints and solids for quilt-top
- 11″ × 11″ (28 cm × 28 cm) of light-colored cotton fabric for the background of the rose medallion
- Template cardboard or plastic
- Bias tape of finished width ½″ (1.3 cm) for around the medallion, for finishing the outer edges of the garment, and for making the front ties (optional). 3¼ yards (297 cm) of tape are needed for finishing a medium-sized pattern. Add ¾ yard (68.6 cm) for ties. The medallion's and the garment's outer edges don't have to be finished in the same color material. You can make the bias tape yourself (see Chapter 5).
- Polyester batting: 1 yard (91.4 cm) of 46″ (116.8 cm) wide batting for medium-sized pattern
- Backing material: 1 yard (91.4 cm) of 46″ (116.8 cm) wide fabric for medium-sized pattern
- Sewing thread of colors that match the fabrics
- Basting thread
- Button (optional)
- Embroidery floss (assorted colors)
- Apparel Pattern 1: The Basic Vest (page 115)

Directions

1. Enlarge and adjust the right front bodice and back bodice pieces of Apparel Pattern 1. Add ⅝″ (1.6 cm) seam allowances around each piece, except on the side seams. Make a second copy of the right front bodice to use for the left front bodice.

2. With transparent tape, join the right front part to the back of the vest bodice pattern at the side seams. Join the left front bodice to the other side seam so that the entire pattern is now one piece. Set it aside.

3. Trace the Rose Medallion and triangle templates onto your template material. Cut out the templates. To assure uniformity in the size of the patches, do not add seam allowances to your templates. Make a block of 8 triangles (like Figure 2) to use as a template block for estimating how much material you need.

4. Sketch the block, made of 8 triangles, onto your bodice pattern papers in colored pencils or crayons. Make the design symmetrical for the left and right halves of the bodice. Remember to draw the Rose Medallion onto your sketch also. The Rose Medallion oval should measure about 10⅛″ (25.7 cm) from top to bottom (not including the bias tape around it), and it should be about 8″ wide (20 cm). If you choose to put side stripes under the armholes of the vest (see color photo), include them in your sketch and cut fabric pieces ¼″ larger on each side than they are on your sketch (this gives you the seam allowances). After you have done your sketch, calculate the number of pieces you will need for each color.

5. Calculate the yardage requirements of your quilt. (See "Estimating Yardage Requirements" in Chapter 3.)

6. Preshrink all quilt-top fabrics and backing. Press the fabrics to remove any wrinkles.

7. For each color of quilt-top fabric, trace the correct number of triangle templates onto the fabric. As you trace each piece, add ¼″ (.6 cm) seam allowance around it. Make the number of pieces that you estimated earlier (Step 4).

8. Cut out the quilt-top pieces, one piece at a time, to ensure uniformity in size.

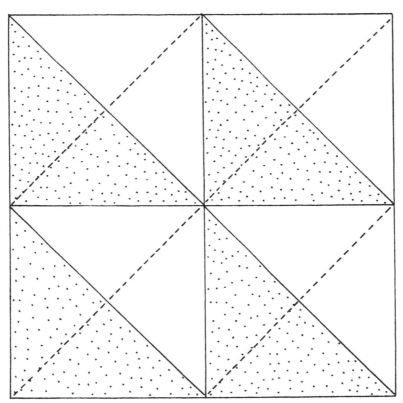

2. Full-sized block made of 8 triangles, which can be used to trace design. Dashed lines show quilting pattern suggested.

9. Piece the blocks together as follows (all piecing is done with right sides of material facing each other):

A. Sew Triangle 1 to Triangle 2 on their long sides. Press seams open after piecing (see Figure 3).

B. Sew the blocks together to form strips (Figure 4). Use your bodice pattern sketches to determine how long each strip should be.

C. Sew the strips together to form the quilt-top fabric. Press all seams open. Set it aside.

10. Cut out an oval about 10⅛″ × 9″ (25.7 cm × 20 cm) for the background of the rose medallion. Refer to the appliqué instructions in Chapter 3 to make the rose design.

A. If you use hand-appliqué, you will need to cut out each rose piece (having added ¼″ seam allowance around each traced template), prepare the individual pieces, and pin and baste the pieces in shape on the medallion background. Then you can appliqué them with satin stitch or buttonhole stitch.

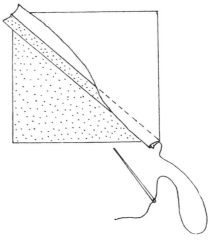

3. Sewing two triangles together to make the pattern.

B. If you plan to do machine appliqué, do not cut out the individual pieces of the rose pattern or of the leaves. Trace the design templates onto your pink and green materials and follow instructions in Chapter 3 for machine appliqué.

11. After the design is appliquéd, iron the entire unit to flatten it. Carefully pin and sew the entire oval in place on the bodice back (see Figure 5).

12. Cut ¾″ (1.9 cm) wide bias tape to encircle the medallion.

13. Fold the edges of the bias tape under and pin the tape in place to cover the seam of the oval medallion. Whipstitch the tape in place around the medallion.

14. Embellish the bias tape with featherstitch embroidery, covering all the seams of the bias tape, to soften the look of the edges.

15. Cut a backing rectangle and batting rectangle about 1″ (2.5 cm) larger on each side than the pieced quilt-top (see Figure 5). Do not cut the backing or batting to shape yet, however.

16. Following the basting instructions in Chapter 3, baste the quilt-top, batting, and backing together for the bodice, using a single thickness of thread.

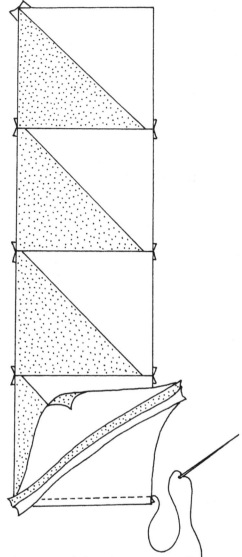

4. Sewing a row of pieced squares together.

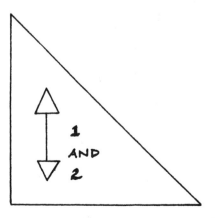

Full-sized triangle template for Rose Medallion Vest.

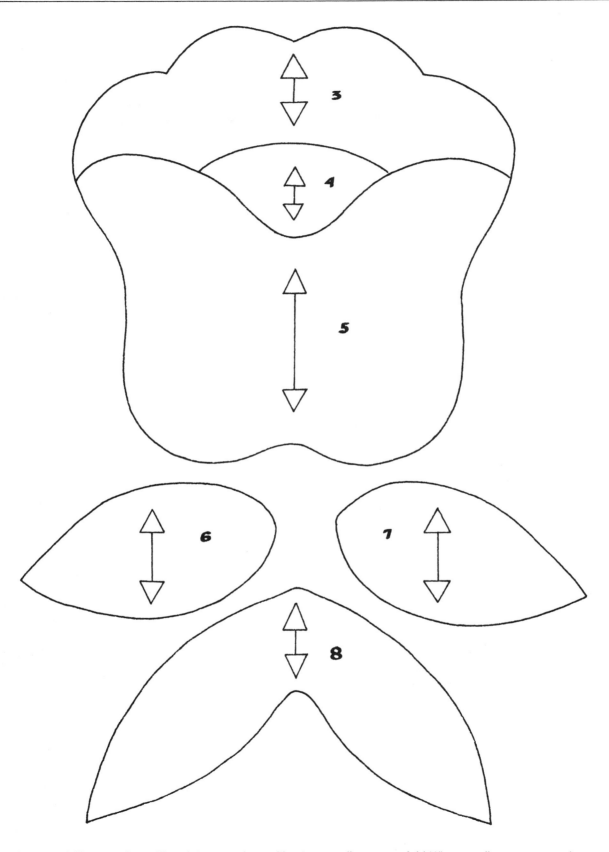

Rose medallion templates. Templates are given without seam allowances. Add ¼" seam allowance around each before cutting material if you are piecing by hand. See color photo for suggested colors.

17. Quilt the vest using diagonal quilting stitches for the strips (see Figure 2 and 5) and outline stitching for the rose motif. Quilt the background of the rose medallion with quilting stitches of your choice.

18. Remove the basting after you have finished quilting.

19. Draw the bodice apparel pattern on the quilted material (Figure 5). Be sure to center the medallion on the back.

20. Set your sewing machine to its largest stitch and stay-stitch ⅟₁₆″ (.16 cm) outside the pattern sewing lines. This will prevent the quilting stitches from coming out after you cut the quilt to shape.

21. Cut out the bodice unit from the pieced material.

22. Construct the vest according to directions in Apparel Pattern 1. (You can skip Step 2 as the side seams already are joined.)

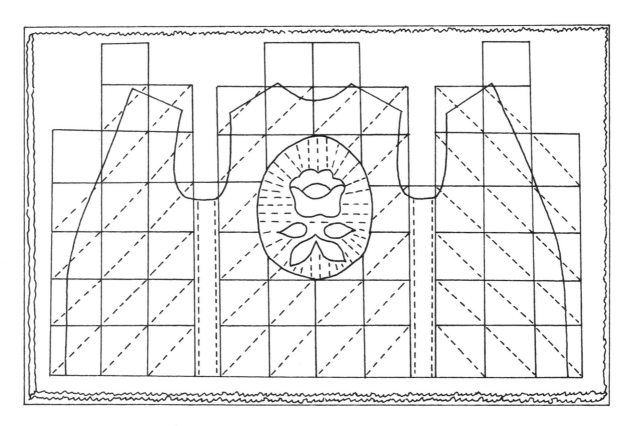

5. The quilting layout of the bodice, showing the position of the Rose Medallion and the optional stripes. Batting and backing are cut in a larger rectangle than the pieced quilt-top. Diagonal lines are quilting lines.

Windmill Vest

1. Windmill Vest, front and back views.

The windmill pattern is a striking design element in a quilt (see Figure 1 and color page E). To heighten the dramatic effect, use contrasting neutrals such as black and white or a dark color and light color. For this project, each apparel pattern section is pieced and quilted separately. These sections are the right front bodice, the left front bodice, and the back bodice.

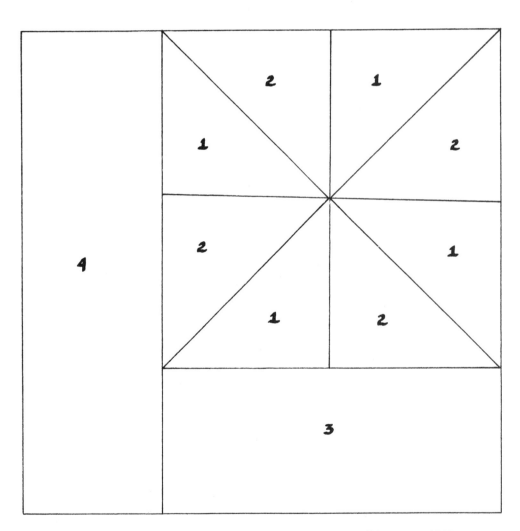

2. Full-sized Windmill Block. Finished size = 5″ × 5″ (12.7 cm × 12.7 cm) without seam allowances.

Birds of Paradise Jacket,
back and front views.

A

Far left: Four-Patch
Variation Vest.
Left: Meandering
Vines Vest.

Near right: Trip Around
the World Vest.
Far right: Strip-Quilt Vest.

B

Crazy-Quilt Kimono Jacket.

Center Diamond Jacket.

Left: Rose Medallion Vest. Right: Windmill Vest.

Left: Honeycomb Quilt Vest. Right: Sawtooth Vest.

Drunkard's Path Jacket.

Octagon Star Jacket.

Materials

- Light-colored cotton fabric
- Dark-colored cotton fabric
- Polyester batting: 2 yards (182.8 cm) of 46″ (116.8 cm) wide batting for medium size
- Backing material: 2 yards (182.8 cm) of 46″ (116.8 cm) wide fabric for medium size
- Bias tape of ½″ (1.3 cm) finishcd width (unfolded width = 2″ (5.1 cm) (You may make this of your own fabric.) For finishing, 3¼ yards (297 cm); for ties, ¾ yard (68.6 cm) of bias tape
- Sewing thread: 1 spool dark; 1 spool light
- Quilting thread: 1 spool dark; 1 spool light
- Basting thread
- Button (optional) or other closure for vest
- Template cardboard or plastic
- Apparel Pattern 4: Oversized Vest (page 126)

Directions

All piecing is done with right sides of material together, unless otherwise noted. Press seams open after each new piece is added.

1. Enlarge and adjust Apparel Pattern 4, the Oversized Vest. (See Chapter 4 for enlarging and adjusting information.) Add ⅝″ (1.6 cm) seam allowance to the pattern sections on all sides except on fold lines. Make a second copy of the right front bodice pattern and reverse it for the left front bodice pattern. Set the pattern papers aside.

2. Transfer the patchwork pattern templates to template material and cut them out. Do not add seam allowances to your templates, to assure uniformity of size. Also make a template of the Windmill Block (Figure 2) for use in Step 3.

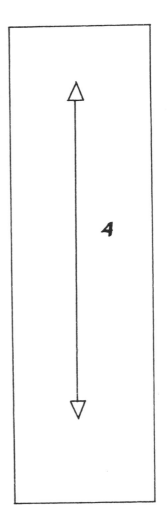

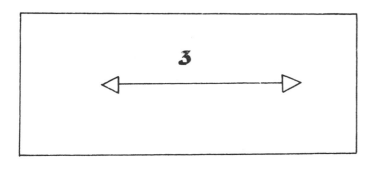

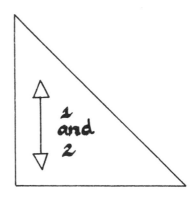

Full-sized templates for the Windmill Block.

3. Determine the number of blocks you will need by directly sketching the Windmill blocks onto your enlarged, adjusted pattern section papers with colored pencils or crayons. Place the right and left front bodice designs symmetrically so that the designs will align across on the finished garment. If you want to include a solid border at the armhole edge and at the bodice front, as shown in Figure 1 and in the color photo of the Windmill Vest, draw pieces 1½″ (3.8 cm) wide for the solid borders on your sketch also. (When you cut out these pieces, you will need to add seam allowances of ¼″ around them.) Multiply the total number of blocks you need by the number of pieces of each size and color in each block, to estimate the total number of patchwork pieces you will need to cut of each size and color (see Chapter 3 for details of these calculations).

4. Calculate the yardage requirements of your quilt-top (see the section on "Estimating Yardage Requirements" in Chapter 3), and get material.

5. Preshrink all quilt-top fabrics, backing material, and bias tape. Press the fabrics to remove wrinkles.

6. Trace the templates onto your quilt-top fabrics (see "Tracing and Cutting the Quilt-Top Patterns" in Chapter 3). Add ¼″ (.6 cm) seam allowances around each piece as you trace it onto your fabric. Trace the number of pieces you need for each color and size, which you calculated in Step 3. If you are planning solid border strips at the armholes and bodice front closing, trace them onto your fabrics also, adding ¼″ seam allowances around them.

7. Cut the patchwork pieces out one at a time to ensure uniformity.

8. To piece the Windmill Block (Figure 2):
   A. Sew Triangle 1 to Triangle 2 on their long sides (Figure 3). For each Windmill Block, you will need 4 pieced squares like the one you just made, so make 3 more.
   B. Join two pieced squares as shown in Figure 4 to make the Windmill square part of the block.
   C. Join Rectangle 3 to the pieced square at the bottom (Figure 5).
   D. Attach Rectangle 4 to the unit you made in Step C on the side of the Windmill square (Figure 6).

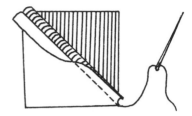

3. Seam a dark and a light triangle together.

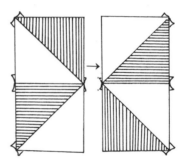

4. Take two rows of two blocks each and join them to make a Windmill square.

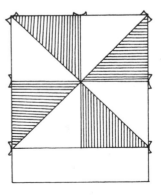

5. Attach Rectangle 3 to the Windmill square.

9. Repeat the block-piecing process given in Step 8 until you have completed the required number of blocks for all three pattern pieces (consult your sketches).

10. Next you will be joining the blocks to make the pieced material that forms the quilt-top. Make the quilt-top for each bodice section separately. Consult the sketches you made on each pattern piece to see how long the rows of blocks should be for each row, and join the Windmill Blocks into rows as shown in Figure 7. Then join the rows to make the quilt-top for each bodice section (Figure 8). If you are adding the solid-colored border strips, sew them on also.

11. Take the three pieces of quilt-top material you made in Step 10. For each piece, cut a rectangle of batting and a rectangle of backing. The rectangles should be 1″ (2.5 cm) larger on each side than your pieced material for that section.

12. With one thickness of thread, baste the quilt-top fabric for each bodice piece to the batting and backing rectangles you cut for that bodice piece. See instructions on basting in Chapter 3. Remember to baste away from the center of each pattern piece to smooth out the fabric surface.

13. Quilt each of the basted bodice pieces separately, using outline stitching (see Chapter 3 for "Common Quilting Stitches"). Use light-colored thread for the light-colored patches and dark-colored thread for the dark patches. Remove the basting threads.

14. Transfer your enlarged, adjusted apparel patterns to the quilted bodice sections.

15. Set your sewing machine on its largest stitch and stay-stitch ¹⁄₁₆″ (.16 cm) outside the seam lines on each bodice piece. This will prevent the quilted fabric from coming apart after you cut the pieces to shape.

16. Carefully cut out the bodice pieces along the cutting lines.

17. Construct the vest according to the directions in Apparel Pattern 4, starting at Step 3. Make bias ties to hold the front sections together, if you wish, or use a button and a roulou loop (see Chapter 5 for roulou loops).

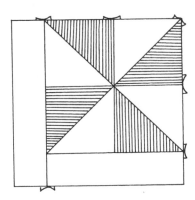

6. Attach Rectangle 4 to the Windmill square to form the completed Windmill Block.

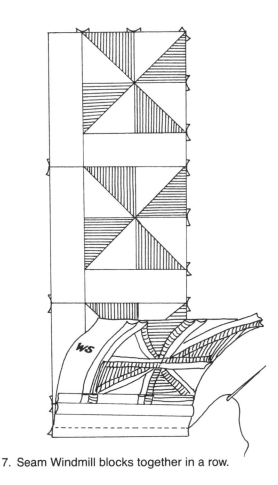

7. Seam Windmill blocks together in a row.

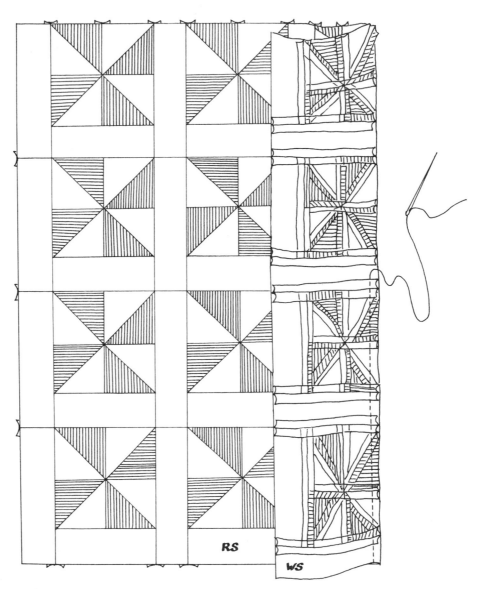

8. Seam rows of Windmill blocks together to make the quilt-top fabric.

Center Diamond Jacket

1. Center Diamond Jacket, front and back views.

The Center Diamond pattern, found mostly in Amish quilts, has geometric simplicity of design. The Center Diamond Jacket allows for piecing of medium-weight fabrics, which is practical for a garment for everyday use. For this project, each quilted section of the apparel pattern is pieced and quilted separately; these are the right front bodice, the left front bodice, the back bodice, and the sleeves. See color page D.

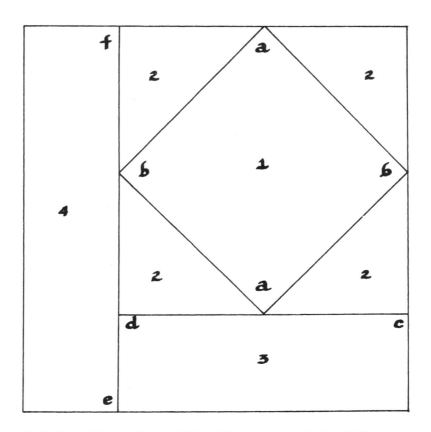

2. Full-sized Center Diamond Block. The block size is 4″ × 4″ (10 cm × 10 cm) without seam allowances.

Materials

- Medium-dark solid-colored cotton fabric (for diamonds)
- Light-colored printed or solid-colored cotton fabric (for background of diamonds)
- Dark-colored cotton fabric (for cuffs, collar, and rectangles between diamond squares)
- Polyester batting: 2 yards (182.8 cm) of 46" (116.8 cm) wide batting for all sizes
- Backing fabric: 2 yards (182.8 cm) of 46" (116.8 cm) wide fabric for all sizes
- 3 yards (274.2 cm) of bias tape of ½" (1.3 cm) finished width; unfolded width = 2" (5.1 cm). (You may make this of your own fabric.)
- Interfacing for collar and cuffs
- Sewing thread; match the colors with the fabrics
- Quilting thread; match the colors with the fabrics
- Basting thread
- Button (optional) to close jacket
- Template cardboard or plastic
- Apparel Pattern 5: Tailored Jacket (page 130)

Directions

All piecing is done with right sides of material together, unless otherwise noted. Press seams open after each new piece is added.

1. Enlarge and adjust Apparel Pattern 5, the Tailored Jacket. See Chapter 4 for enlarging and adjusting information. Add ⅝" (1.6 cm) seam allowance to the pattern sections on all sides except on fold lines. Make a second copy of the right front bodice and reverse it for the left front bodice pattern. Set the pattern papers aside.

2. Transfer the patchwork pattern templates to template material and cut them out. Do not add seam allowances to your templates, to assure uniformity of size. Also make a template of the Center Diamond Block (Figure 2).

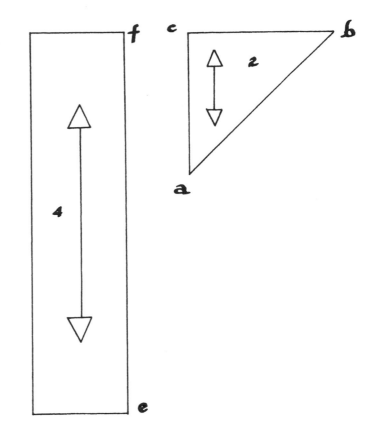

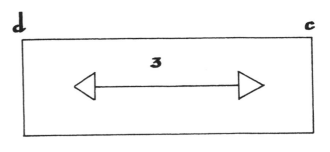

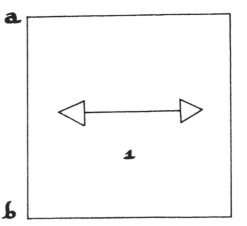

Full-sized templates for the Center Diamond Block. Seam allowances are not included.

3. Determine the number of blocks you will need by directly sketching the Center Diamond blocks onto your enlarged, adjusted pattern section papers with colored pencils or crayons. Place the right and left front bodice designs symmetrically so that the designs will align across on the finished garment. Multiply the total number of blocks you need by the number of pieces of each size and color in each block, to estimate the total number of patchwork pieces you will need to cut of each size and color (see Chapter 3 for details of these calculations).

4. Calculate the yardage requirements of your quilt-top (see the section on "Estimating Yardage Requirements" in Chapter 3), and get material.

5. Preshrink all quilt-top fabrics, backing material, and bias tape. Press the fabrics to remove wrinkles.

6. Trace the templates onto your patchwork fabrics (see "Tracing and Cutting the Quilt-Top Patterns" in Chapter 3). Add ¼″ (.6 cm) seam allowances around each piece as you trace it onto your fabric. Trace the number of pieces you need for each color and size, which you calculated in Step 3.

7. Cut the patchwork pieces out one at a time to ensure uniformity.

8. To piece the Center Diamond Block (Figure 2):
   A. Form a pieced square by joining four of Triangle 2 around Square 1, sewing each triangle from a to b, as illustrated in Figure 3.
   B. Attach Rectangle 3 to the pieced square from d to c, as shown in Figure 4.
   C. Attach Rectangle 4 from f to e, as shown in Figure 5.

9. Repeat the block-piecing process given in Step 8 until you have completed the required number of blocks for all five pattern pieces (consult your sketches).

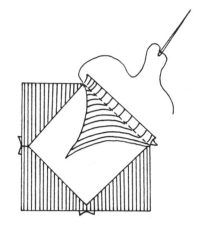

3. Seaming triangles to the center diamond.

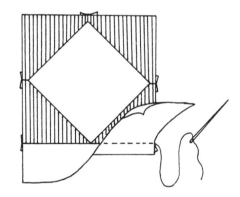

4. Attach Rectangle 3 to the pieced square.

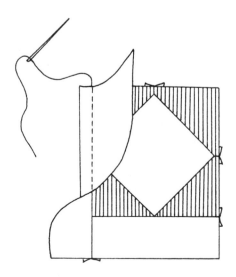

5. Attach Rectangle 4.

10. Next you will be joining the blocks to make the pieced material that forms the quilt-top. Make the quilt-top for each quilted pattern section separately. Consult the sketches on each pattern piece to see how long the rows of blocks should be for each row, and join the Center Diamond blocks into rows as shown in Figure 6. Then join the rows to make the quilt-top for each quilted section, using your sketches on your pattern pieces for reference.

11. Take the five quilted pieces you made in Step 10. For each piece, cut a rectangle of batting and a rectangle of backing. The rectangles should be 1″ (2.5 cm) larger on each side than your quilt-top piece.

12. With one thickness of thread, baste the quilt-top fabric for each pattern piece to be quilted to the batting and backing rectangles you cut in Step 11. See instructions on basting in Chapter 3. Remember to baste away from the center of each pattern piece to smooth out the fabric surface.

13. Quilt each of the basted pieces separately, using outline stitching. Add criss-crossed vertical and horizontal quilting lines (Figure 7) to hold the fabric flat against the batting. Remove the basting after quilting.

14. Transfer your apparel patterns of the right front bodice, left front bodice, back bodice, and the sleeves to the quilted sections.

15. Set your sewing machine on its largest stitch and stay-stitch 1⁄16″ (.16 cm) outside the seam lines on each quilted pattern piece. This will prevent the quilted fabric from coming apart after you cut the pieces to shape.

16. Carefully cut out the quilted pieces along the cutting lines.

17. Construct the jacket according to the directions in Apparel Pattern 5 (Tailored Jacket), starting at Step 2. Make a roulou loop to hold the front sections together (see Chapter 5), if you wish, and attach a button below the collar (see Figure 1).

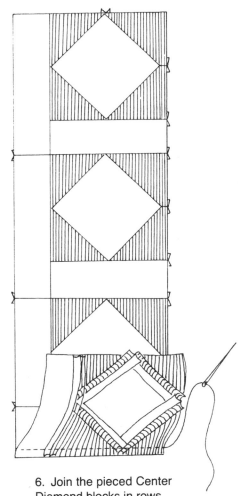

6. Join the pieced Center Diamond blocks in rows.

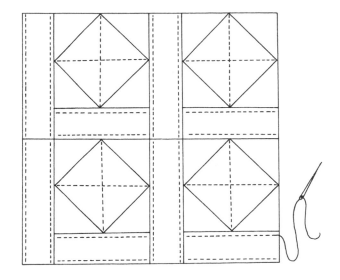

7. Quilting pattern for the Center Diamond blocks.

Trip Around the World Vest

1. Trip Around the World Vest, front and back views.

The placement of dark and light fabrics of varying degrees of values and intensities is the main design element in this vest (Figure 1 and color page B). Trip Around the World, also known as Sunshine and Shadow, is a quilt-top pattern most suitable for dramatic effects. The selection of the color scheme and placement of the patches dictate the overall effect of the garment. (See figures 2 and 3 for variations.)

Materials

- Scrap fabrics of light and dark colors
- Backing material: 2 yards (182.8 cm) of 46" (116.8 cm) wide fabric for all sizes
- Polyester batting: 2 yards (182.8 cm) of 46" (116.8 cm) wide batting for all sizes
- Sewing thread: 1 spool light color, 1 spool dark
- Quilting thread: 1 spool light color, 1 spool dark
- 4¼ yards (388.5 cm) of bias tape of ½" (1.3 cm) finished width; unfolded width = 2" (5.1 cm). (You may make this of your own fabric.)
- Covered shank button (optional)
- Basting thread
- Template cardboard or plastic
- Apparel Pattern 4: Oversized Vest (page 126)

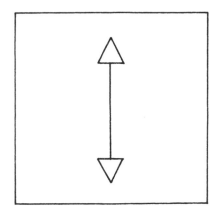

Full-sized template for the Trip Around the World Vest. The template does not include seam allowances.

Directions

All piecing is done with right sides of material together, unless otherwise noted. Press seams open after each new piece is added.

1. Enlarge and adjust Apparel Pattern 4, the Oversized Vest. See Chapter 4 for enlarging and adjusting information. Add ⅝" (1.6 cm) seam allowance to the pattern sections on all sides except on fold lines. Make a second copy of the right front bodice and reverse it for the left front bodice pattern. Join the front bodice pattern pieces to the back bodice pattern at the shoulders (Figure 4). Set the pattern paper aside.

2. Transfer the patchwork pattern template to template cardboard or plastic and cut it out. Do not add seam allowances to your template, to assure uniformity of size.

3. Determine the number of blocks you will need by directly sketching the Trip Around the World pattern onto your enlarged, adjusted pattern paper with colored pencils or crayons. Place the right and left front bodice designs symmetrically so that the designs will align across on the finished garment. Estimate the total number of patchwork pieces you will need to cut of each color (see Chapter 3 for details of these calculations). If you place the darker patches toward the outer parts of the vest and the lighter patches toward the face, it will have a more slimming effect than if you place the light-colored patches on the outside edges.

4. Calculate the yardage requirements of your quilt-top (see the section on "Estimating

2. Different effects are achieved by varying the placement of the patches in the Trip Around the World Vest.

3. Two additional variations in placement of the patches, for the Trip Around the World Vest.

Yardage Requirements" in Chapter 3), and get material.

5. Preshrink all quilt-top fabrics, backing material, and bias tape. Press the fabrics to remove wrinkles.

6. Trace the template onto your quilt-top fabrics (see "Tracing and Cutting the Quilt-Top Patterns" in Chapter 3). Add ¼" (.6 cm) seam allowances around each piece as you trace it onto your fabric. Trace the number of pieces you need for each color, which you calculated in Step 3.

7. Cut the patchwork pieces out one at a time to ensure uniformity.

8. Before sewing the patches together, lay out all the pieces on your pattern paper and view the overall effect of the diamonds (see Figure 5). Positioning the tips of the diamonds at the hem of the vest enhances the aesthetic effect.

9. Sew the patches together to form the quilt-top material. Positioning rows of squares in a diagonal formation will make this task simpler and faster (see Figure 6). Don't cut out the vest yet, however.

10. Cut a rectangle of batting and a rectangle of backing. The rectangles should be 1" (2.5 cm) larger on each side than your pieced quilt-top material.

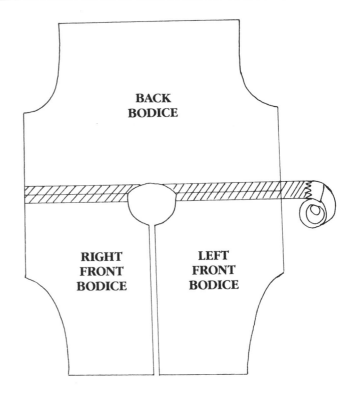

4. Tape the front vest patterns to the back vest pattern at the seams.

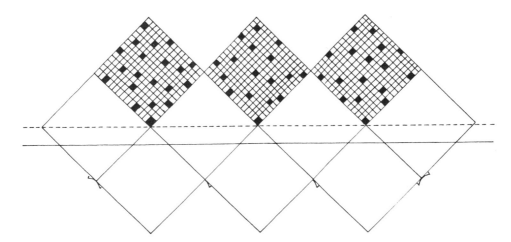

5. Positioning the tops of the diamonds at the hem of the vest enchances the aesthetic effect. Dashed line is hemline.

6. Piecing layout of the quilt-top. Sew diagonal strips, then join them.

11. With one thickness of thread, baste together the pieced quilt-top fabric, and the batting rectangle, and backing rectangle you cut in Step 10. See instructions on basting in Chapter 3. Baste away from the center of the piece to smooth out the fabric surface.

12. Quilt the vest material you basted together in Step 11, using outline stitching (see page 34). Remove the basting after quilting is done.

13. Transfer your apparel pattern to the quilted material.

14. Set your sewing machine on its largest stitch and stay-stitch $1/16''$ (.16 cm) outside the seam lines of the entire vest. This will prevent the quilted fabric from coming apart after you cut the vest to shape.

15. Carefully cut out the quilted vest along the cutting lines.

16. Construct the vest according to the directions in Apparel Pattern 4 (Oversized Vest), starting at Step 3. Make a roulou loop (see Chapter 5) to hold the front sections together, if you wish, and attach a button at the top of the front opening (see Figure 1).

Sawtooth Vest

1. Sawtooth Vest, front and back views.

One of the most interesting geometric quilt designs is the Sawtooth. The pattern is created by arranging dark and light triangles in a square block. The jagged edges in the design can be emphasized by using contrasting colors, or they can be softened by using pastel colors (see color page F). The vest consists of three sections: the right front bodice, the left front bodice, and the back bodice.

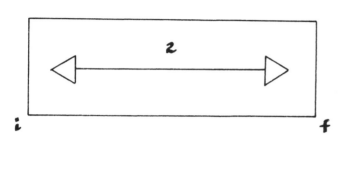

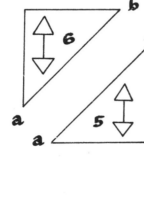

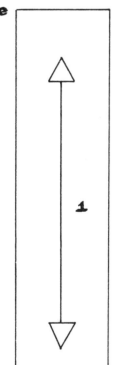

Full-sized templates for the Sawtooth Block. Seam allowances are not included.

Materials

- Light-colored cotton fabric
- Dark-colored solid or print cotton fabric
- Backing fabric: 1 yard (91.4 cm) of 46″ (116.8 cm) wide fabric for medium-sized pattern
- Polyester batting: 1 yard (91.4 cm) of 46″ (116.8 cm) wide batting for medium-sized pattern
- 3¼ yards (297 cm) of bias tape of ½″ (1.3 cm) finished width; unfolded width = 2″ (5.1 cm). (You may make this of your own fabric or purchase them.)
- Sewing thread: match quilt-top fabrics' colors
- Quilting thread: 1 spool light; 1 spool dark
- Basting thread
- Template cardboard or plastic
- Button (optional)
- Apparel Pattern 1: Basic Vest (page 115)

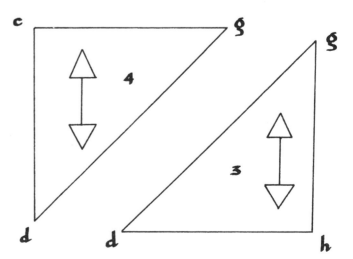

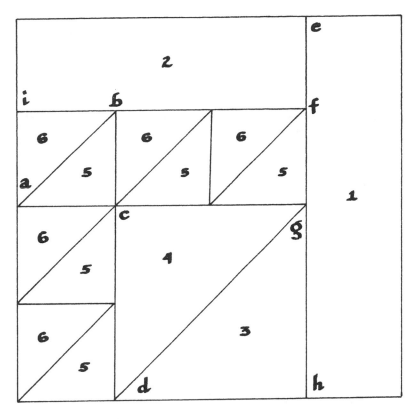

2. Full-sized Sawtooth Block. Block is 4⅛″ × 4⅛″ (10.4 cm × 10.4 cm) without seam allowances.

Directions

All piecing is done with right sides of material together, unless otherwise noted. Press seams open after each new piece is added.

1. Enlarge and adjust Apparel Pattern 1, the Basic Vest. See Chapter 4 for enlarging and adjusting information. Add ⅝″ (1.6 cm) seam allowance to the pattern sections on all sides. Make a second copy of the right front bodice pattern and reverse it for the left front bodice pattern. Set the pattern papers aside.

2. Transfer the patchwork pattern templates to template cardboard or plastic and cut them out. Do not add seam allowances to your templates, to assure uniformity of size. Also make a template of the Sawtooth Block (Figure 2).

3. Determine the number of blocks you will need by directly sketching the Sawtooth blocks onto your enlarged, adjusted pattern section papers with colored pencils or crayons. Place the right and left front bodice designs symmetrically so that the designs will align across on the finished garment. If you want to include a solid-colored strip on the front bodice, as shown in the color photo of the Sawtooth Vest, draw the strips on your sketches also. Multiply the total number of blocks you need by the number of pieces of each size and color in each block, to estimate the total number of patchwork pieces you will need to cut of each size and color (see Chapter 3 for details of these calculations).

4. Calculate the yardage requirements of your quilt-top (see the section on "Estimating Yardage Requirements" in Chapter 3), and get material.

5. Preshrink all quilt-top fabrics, backing material, and bias tape. Press the fabrics to remove wrinkles.

6. Trace the templates onto your patchwork fabrics (see "Tracing and Cutting the Quilt-Top Patterns" in Chapter 3). Add ¼″ (.6 cm) seam allowances around each piece as you trace it onto your fabric. Trace the number of pieces you need for each color and size, which you

calculated in Step 3. If you are planning solid strips on the bodice front, trace them onto your fabrics also, adding ¼″ seam allowances around them.

7. Cut the patchwork pieces out one at a time to ensure uniformity.

8. To piece the Sawtooth Block (Figure 2):
   A. Create a large pieced square by sewing Triangle 4 to Triangle 3 from g to d (Figure 3).
   B. Create a small square by joining Triangle 6 to Triangle 5 by sewing from a to b (Figure 4). Make four more small squares the same way.
   C. Join three small squares from Step B in a row (Figure 5).
   D. Join two small squares from Step B in another row (Figure 6).
   E. Attach the row of two small pieced squares from Step D to the large pieced square you made in Step A, by sewing from c to g. Position Triangle 4 as shown in Figure 7.

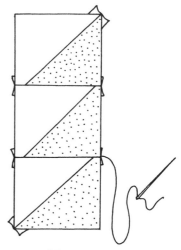

5. Make a row of three small pieced squares.

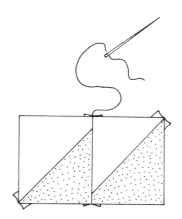

6. Make a row of two small pieced squares.

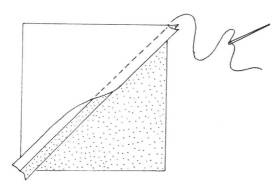

3. Sew together two large triangles to make a large pieced square.

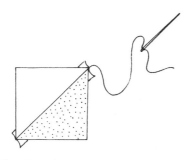

4. Sew together two small triangles to make a small pieced square.

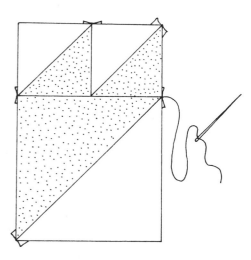

7. Attach the row of two small pieced squares to the large pieced square.

F. By sewing from b to d, attach the row of three small squares from Step C to the unit you made in Step E (see Figure 8).

G. By sewing from i to f, join Rectangle 2 to the unit you made in Step F (Figure 9).

H. By sewing from e to h, join Rectangle 1 to the unit you made in Step G (Figure 10).

9. Repeat the block-piecing process given in Step 8 until you have completed the required number of blocks for all three bodice pattern pieces (consult your sketches).

10. Next you will be joining the blocks to make the pieced material that forms the quilt-top. Make the quilt-top material for each bodice section separately. Consult the sketches you made on each pattern piece to see how long the rows of blocks should be for each row, and join the blocks into rows (Figure 11). Then join the rows to make the quilt-top for each bodice section. If you are adding the solid-colored strips, sew them on also. Don't cut out the pattern pieces yet, however.

11. Take the three pieces of quilt-top material you made in Step 10. For each piece, cut a rectangle of batting and a rectangle of backing. Each rectangle should be 1″ (2.5 cm) larger on each side than your quilt-top pieced material for that pattern section.

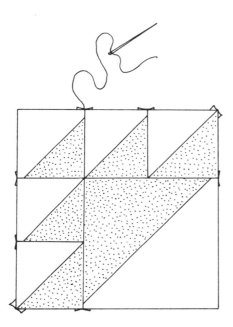

8. Attach the row of three small pieced squares as shown.

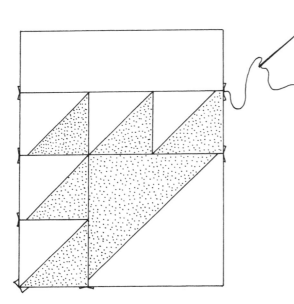

9. Attach Rectangle 2 as shown.

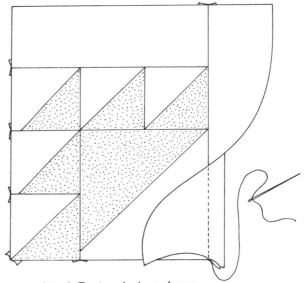

10. Attach Rectangle 1 as shown.

12. With one thickness of thread, baste the quilt-top fabric for each bodice piece to the batting and backing rectangles you cut for that bodice piece. See instructions on basting in Chapter 3. Remember to baste away from the center of each pattern piece to smooth out the fabric surface.

13. Quilt each of the basted bodice material pieces separately, using outline stitching (see Figure 12). Use light-colored thread for the light-colored patches and dark-colored thread for the dark-colored patches. Remove basting threads after quilting is finished.

14. Transfer your enlarged, adjusted apparel patterns to the quilted bodice material sections.

15. Set your sewing machine on its largest stitch and stay-stitch 1/16″ (.16 cm) outside the seam lines on each bodice piece. This will prevent the quilted fabric from coming apart after you cut the pieces to shape.

16. Carefully cut out the bodice pieces along the cutting lines.

17. Construct the vest according to the directions in Apparel Pattern 1, starting at Step 2. If you wish, make and attach a roulou loop (see Chapter 5), and attach a button to close the vest, as shown in Figure 1 and in the color photo.

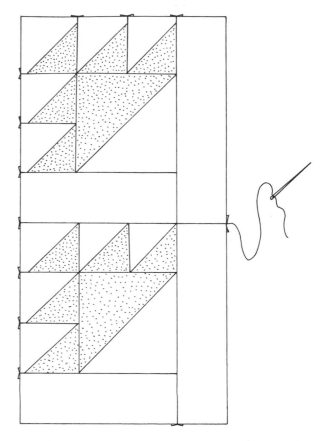

11. Join two Sawtooth blocks as shown to make the pattern.

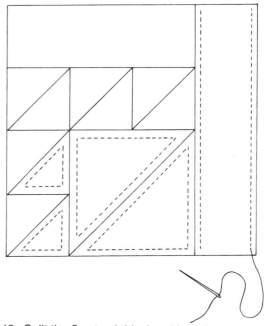

12. Quilt the Sawtooth blocks with outline stitching.

Four-Patch Variation Vest

1. Four-Patch Variation Vest, front and back views.

The versatility of the four-patch pattern is demonstrated in the Four-Patch Variation Vest. The blocks on the bodice front are placed in an angled position so that the squares form a cluster of diamonds within diamonds. Bias tapes of varying widths emphasize the central motif on the back of the vest (see Figure 1). In our model, the earth-toned shades of browns and beiges subtly impart a rustic flair to the design (see color page B). Of course, you can choose other color combinations if your prefer to do so. The vest is a perfect choice for classic dressing. For this project, each apparel pattern section is pieced and quilted separately: the right front bodice, the left front bodice, and the back bodice.

Materials

- Brown, white, and beige cotton fabrics
- Dark-colored printed cotton fabric scraps
- Polyester batting: 1 yard (91.4 cm) of 46″ (116.8 cm) wide batting for medium-sized pattern
- Backing material: 1 yard (91.4 cm) of 46″ (116.8 cm) wide fabric for medium-sized pattern
- Button (optional)
- Bias tapes whose unfolded widths are 1″ (2.5 cm) and 3″ (7.6 cm) for appliqué and 3¼ yards (297 cm) of 2″ (5.1 cm) wide bias tape for finishing (finished width = ½″ [1.3 cm]). Add ¾ yard (68.6 cm) of 2″ wide tape for ties if desired. You may make these from fabric or purchase them.
- Sewing thread: 1 spool dark; 1 spool light
- Quilting thread: 1 spool dark; 1 spool light
- Basting thread
- Template cardboard or plastic
- Apparel Pattern #1: Basic Vest (page 115)

2. Reduced piecing diagram of four-patch block plus large square, for front bodice sections.

Directions

All piecing is done with right sides of material together, unless otherwise noted. Press seams open after each new piece is added.

1. Enlarge and adjust Apparel Pattern 1, the Basic Vest. See Chapter 4 for enlarging and adjusting information. Add ⅝″ (1.6 cm) seam allowance to the pattern sections on all sides. Make a second copy of the right bodice front and reverse it for the left bodice front pattern. Set the pattern papers aside.

2. Transfer the patchwork pattern templates to template cardboard or plastic and cut them out. Do not add seam allowances to your templates, to assure uniformity of size.

3. Determine the number of blocks you will need by directly tracing the templates of the four-patch design and Square 3 onto your enlarged, adjusted pattern section papers for the front bodice pieces with colored pencils or crayons. Place the right and left bodice front designs symmetrically so that the designs will align across on the finished garment (see Figure 1 and the color photo of the Four-Patch Vest for guidance). Multiply the total number of blocks you need by the number of pieces of each size and color in each block, to estimate the total number of patchwork pieces you will need to cut of each size and color (see Chapter 3 for details of these calculations) for the bodice fronts. For the back bodice, you will need 5 four-patch blocks, four of Triangle 4, and four of Triangle 5. (See Figure 1 for sketch of back bodice). You may want to use the same color material for Square 3, the bias tape, and the vest's backing material (lining) to ensure a good color transition from the front of the bodice to the back of the bodice.

4. Calculate the yardage requirements of your quilt-top (see the section on "Estimating Yardage Requirements" in Chapter 3), and get material.

5. Preshrink all quilt-top fabrics, backing material, and bias tape. Press the fabrics to remove wrinkles.

6. Trace the templates onto your patchwork fabrics (see "Tracing and Cutting the Quilt-Top Patterns" in Chapter 3). Add ¼" (.6 cm) seam allowances around each piece as you trace it onto your fabric. Trace the number of pieces you need for each color and size, which you calculated in Step 3.

7. Cut the patchwork pieces out one at a time to ensure uniformity.

8. To piece the Four-Patch Block plus Square (Figure 2):
A. Join Square 1 and Square 2 from a to b (Figure 3) to form a pieced rectangle, maintaining the same grainline direction across both squares. Repeat this to make another pieced rectangle.

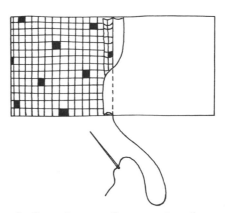

3. Seam two small squares together.

B. Sew the two pieced rectangles together to form the four-patch block (Figure 4). Remember to press seams open as you sew.

C. Join the four-patch block to Square 3 as shown in Figure 5.

D. Refer to your sketches in Step 3 and make as many four-patch blocks with large squares attached as you need to be enough for your bodice fronts.

E. Following your colored sketches on the bodice front, join the pieced units you made in Step 8D on the diagonal (see Figure 1), to form the material for the bodice front. Do not cut out the bodice fronts yet, however.

9. To make the central diamond of the back bodice, first study Figure 6, a diagram of the material you need to piece for the back bodice (Figure 11 shows how the pattern will fit on the material). Then:

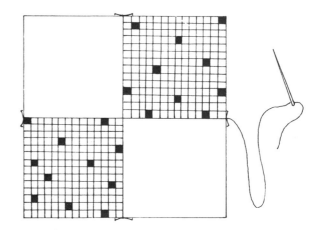

4. Join two rows of two small squares each to make the Four-Patch Block.

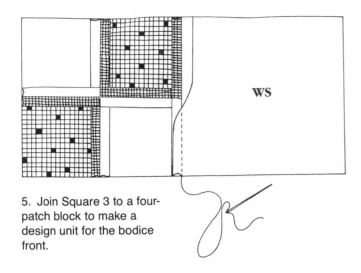

5. Join Square 3 to a four-patch block to make a design unit for the bodice front.

A. Make 5 four-patch blocks, as you did in Step 8B, for the central diamond design for the back.

B. Sew a Triangle 4 from h to i onto a four-patch block (see Figure 7). Sew another Triangle 4 on the opposite side of the four-patch block. Set the unit aside.

C. Make another unit exactly the same as the one you made in Step 9B.

D. Join 3 four-patch units in a row, as shown in Figure 8. Sew from f to g to attach a Triangle 5 to one end of the row of blocks. Add another Triangle 5 to the opposite side of the row. Set the unit aside.

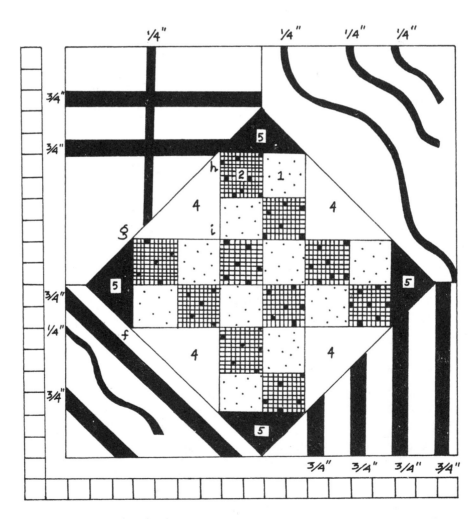

6. Layout for the back of the bodice. Scale: 1 box = 1 in.² (2.5 cm × 2.5 cm). Widths of bias tape are the finished widths (unfolded width is 4 times as wide). Triangular sections will be wider if you enlarged the pattern earlier.

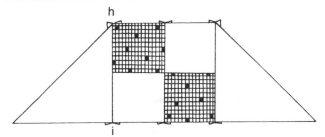

7. Sew a Triangle 4 to each side of a pieced four-patch block as shown.

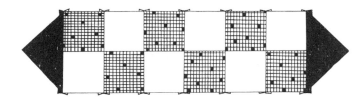

8. Join 3 four-patch blocks in a row; then add a Triangle 5 to each end, as shown.

E. Sew the units you made in steps 9B, 9C, and 9D together, as shown in Figure 9. Add a Triangle 5 at the top and at the bottom. This completes the central diamond of the bodice back.

10. Using a pencil and a ruler, divide the back bodice pattern into four quarters, as shown in Figure 10.

11. Measure the central diamond you made in Step 9. Trace the central diamond motif onto your paper back bodice pattern (see Figure 11 and Figure 6).

12. Trace out one triangular back section onto template cardboard or plastic, and cut it out. Do not add seam allowances to your template (Figure 12).

13. Trace the triangular template onto your background fabric. Add ⅝″ (1.6 cm) seam allowances all around it, except on the side that

will be sewn to the central diamond motif; add ¼″ (.6 cm) seam allowance to the side that will be sewn to the central diamond. Trace the template onto the fabric 3 times more to make the remaining three-quarters of the vest back, for a total of 4 triangular parts, adding seam allowances as for the first quarter. Cut out the fabric triangles and sew them to the center diamond and to each other, using Figure 6 as a guide.

14. Following the layout in Figure 6, position the decorative bias tapes on the back bodice triangles, or use some other design for the bias tapes, if you prefer. Sew them in place.

15. For each pattern piece (the bodice fronts and the bodice back) cut a rectangle of batting and a rectangle of backing. Each rectangle should be 1″ (2.5 cm) larger on each side than your quilt-top pieced material for that pattern section. Do not cut anything to shape yet, however.

16. With one thickness of thread, baste the quilt-top fabric for each bodice piece to the batting and backing rectangles you cut for that bodice piece. See instructions on basting in Chapter 3. Remember to baste away from the center of each pattern piece to smooth out the fabric surface.

17. Quilt each of the basted bodice pieces separately, using outline stitching and vertical and horizontal stitching (see Chapter 3 for "Common Quilting Stitches"). Use light-colored thread for the light-colored patches and dark-colored thread for the dark-colored patches. Remove basting threads after quilting is finished.

18. Transfer your enlarged, adjusted apparel patterns to the quilted bodice sections.

19. Set your sewing machine on its largest stitch and stay-stitch ¹⁄₁₆″ (.16 cm) outside the seam lines on each bodice piece. This will prevent the quilted fabric from coming apart after you cut the pieces to shape.

20. Carefully cut out the bodice pieces along the cutting lines.

21. Construct the vest according to the directions in Apparel Pattern 1, starting at Step 2. If you wish, make and attach ties of bias binding in the front to hold the vest together.

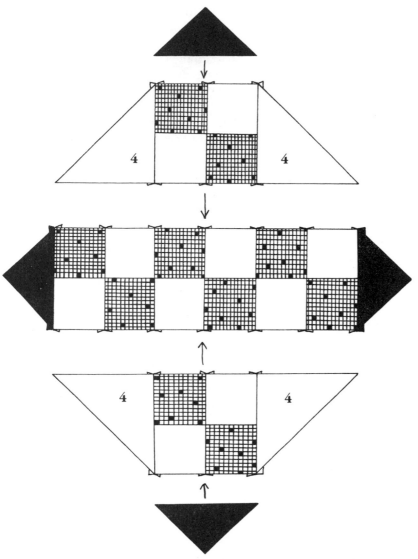

9. Piecing diagram of the central diamond motif of the back bodice.

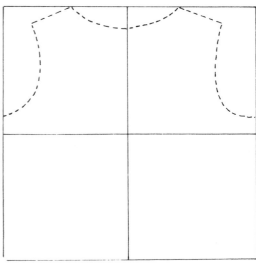

10. With pencil lines, divide your vest back bodice pattern into quarters.

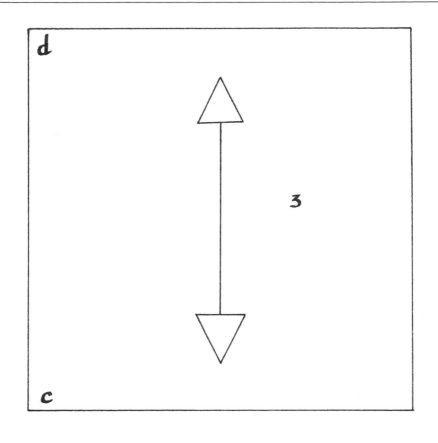

Full-sized templates of the Four-Patch Variation Vest. Seam allowances are not included. Arrows indicate the straight grain of the fabric.

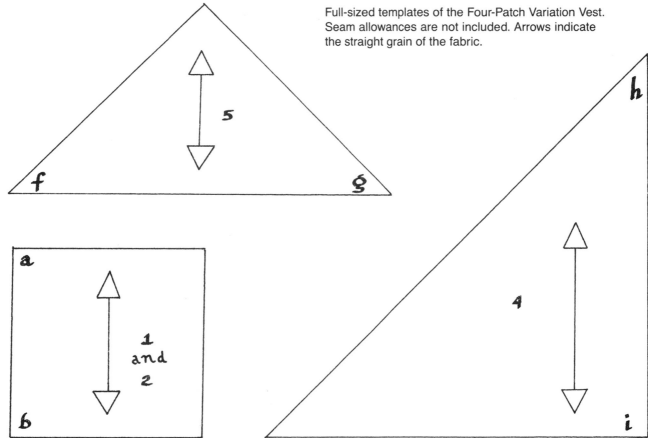

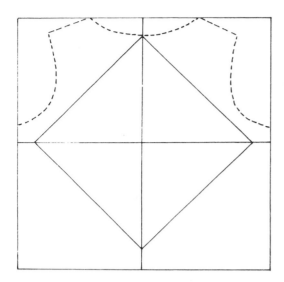

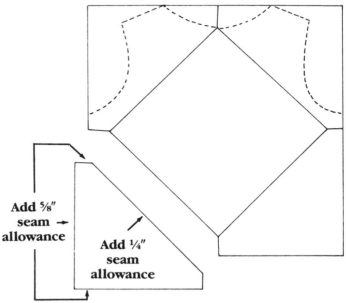

11. Trace the central diamond motif onto the pattern for the vest back. If you adjusted the bodice pattern, the triangular sections around the diamond will be slightly bigger or smaller than in Figure 6. Do not cut out the bodice back yet, however. Dashed line indicates where the pattern will be positioned.

12. Trace one triangular back section from your back bodice pattern and add seam allowances of ⅝″ (1.6 cm) on all sides except the one that joins the diamond shape—add seam allowance of ¼″ (.6 cm) there.

Drunkard's Path Jacket: Birds in Flight Variation

1. Drunkard's Path Jacket, Birds-in-Flight Variation, front and back views.

The Drunkard's Path motif is a fascinating pattern. By simple manipulation of the colors of the block, almost limitless designs can be achieved. When you use the pattern, carefully plan the placement of dark and light patches for the quilt-top. See Figure 1 and the color photo on color page G for examples.

Materials

- Light-colored printed or light solid-colored cotton fabric
- Dark printed or dark solid-colored cotton fabric
- Backing material: 4 yards (365.6 cm) of 46" (116.8 cm) wide fabric for all sizes
- Polyester batting: 4 yards (365.6 cm) of 46" (116.8 cm) wide batting for all sizes
- Sewing thread: light and dark colors to match the quilt-top fabrics
- Quilting thread: light and dark colors to match the quilt-top fabrics
- Basting thread
- 3 yards (274.2 cm) of bias tapes of finished width ½" (1.3 cm); unfolded width is 2" (5.1 cm). You may make the bias tape from your fabric or purchase it
- Interfacing for collar sash and cuffs
- Template cardboard or plastic
- Apparel Pattern 3: Kimono Jacket (page 119)

Directions

1. Take the Kimono Jacket pattern on page 120. Trace out the entire page as one pattern piece, including the right front and back bodice sections and the front and back yokes. Add the cuff section pattern on page 121 to the end of the sleeve pattern. Enlarge and adjust the pattern (see Chapter 4 for enlarging and adjusting instructions).

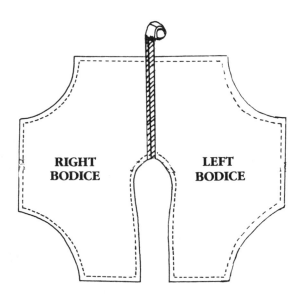

RIGHT BODICE   LEFT BODICE

2. Tape the pattern sections to form one single pattern piece.

2. Trace a copy of the right jacket pattern made in Step 1 and reverse it for the left jacket pattern. Tape the right and left patterns together to create a single main pattern piece (Figure 2). Add ⅝" (1.6 cm) seam allowance around all the edges of the bodice pattern.

3. Transfer the Drunkard's Path patchwork pattern templates to template material and cut them out. Do not add seam allowances to your templates, to assure uniformity of size. Also make a template of the block for the Drunkard's Patch Design in Figure 3. It will be a help in your next step.

4. Determine the number of blocks you will need by directly sketching the Drunkard's path blocks onto your enlarged, adjusted bodice pattern paper, using colored pencils or crayons (see

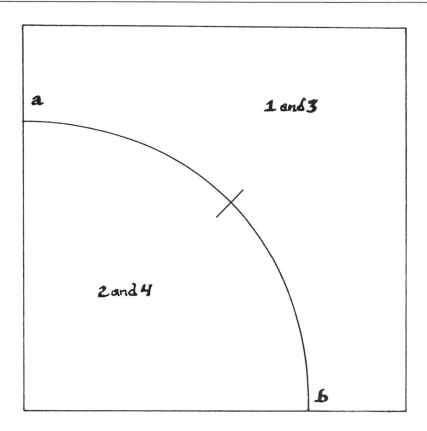

3. Full-sized diagram for the Drunkard's Path block, which is one-quarter of the Birds in Flight Variation. Seam allowances are not included. Block size = 4″ × 4″ (10.2 cm × 10.2 cm).

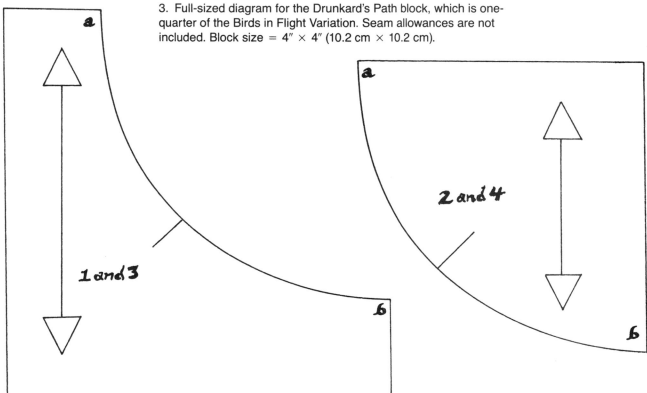

Full-sized templates for the Drunkard's Path block. Seam allowances are not included. Arrows indicate straight grain of fabric.

Figure 7 for guidance). Place the right and left bodice designs symmetrically so that the designs will align across on the finished garment. Estimate the total number of patchwork pieces you will need to cut of each size and color (see Chapter 3 for details of these calculations).

5. Calculate the yardage requirements of your quilt-top (see the section on "Estimating Yardage Requirements" in Chapter 3), and get material.

6. Preshrink all quilt-top fabrics, backing material, and bias tape. Press the fabrics to remove wrinkles.

7. Trace the templates onto your quilt-top fabrics (see "Tracing and Cutting the Quilt-Top Patterns" in Chapter 3). Add ¼″ (.6 cm) seam allowances around each patchwork piece as you trace it onto your fabric. Trace the number of pieces you need for each color and size, which you calculated in Step 4.

8. Cut the patchwork pieces out one at a time to ensure uniformity.

9. To make the Birds-in-Flight Variation of the Drunkard's Path, you will need to piece 4 Drunkard's Path blocks (Figure 3), as shown in Figure 4. Piecing is done with right sides of material together and ¼″ seam allowances, unless otherwise noted.

    A. Sew Piece 3 to Piece 4 from a to b to make the upper left quarter of the pattern. Repeat this for the lower right quarter.

    B. Sew Piece 1 to Piece 2, from a to b, to make the upper right quarter. Repeat this to make the lower left quarter.

    C. To reduce bulk, notch the curved areas of the seam allowances of the pieced quarters up to about ¹⁄₁₆″ (.16 cm) away from the seam lines (see Figure 5). Note: An alternative method of piecing the blocks, using appliqué, is shown in Figure 6. In this method, background squares are cut and the contrasting-colored pieces are appliquéd onto them to make the pattern.

10. After you have made individual blocks in steps 9A–C, join the 4 quarters made in these steps to make the "bird" pattern (see Figure 4). Continue making as many blocks as you need to complete the bodice quilt-top.

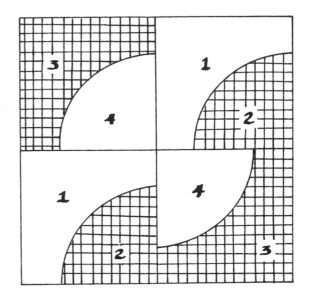

4. Reduced piecing layout for the birds-in-flight variation of the Drunkard's Path design. Pieces 1 and 4 are the same color. Pieces 2 and 3 are the same color.

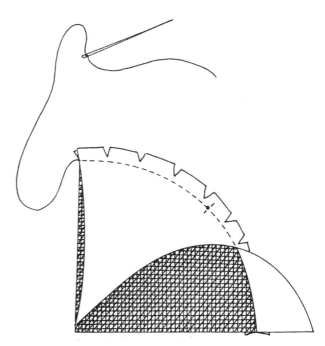

5. Join Piece 1 and 2 (or Piece 3 and Piece 4) by sewing from a to b. Notch seam allowances to keep fabric flat.

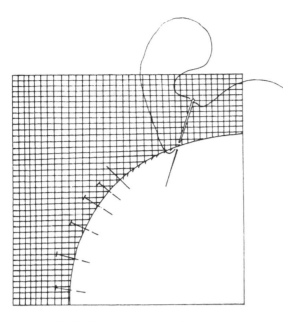

6. Appliqué piecing method.

11. Position the bird motif blocks as you planned in your sketches. See Figure 7 for reference.

12. Join the bird-motif blocks in vertical columns to simplify piecing the quilt-top. Press the seams open after sewing.

13. Iron the surface of the quilt-top after the piecing process is completed. If you use the pieced method described in steps 9A–C, iron the seams open. If you use the appliqué method, iron the entire quilt-top material flat after it is appliquéd.

14. After you have pieced the entire bodice quilt-top, cut the batting and backing material in a rectangle that is 1″ larger on each side than the pieced quilt-top.

15. Baste the quilt-top, batting, and backing layers together (see basting instructions in Chapter 3).

FRONT

BACK

7. Layout of blocks for the quilt-top material.

16. Quilt the layers with outline stitching (see Figure 8).

17. Remove the basting stitches after quilting.

18. Take the paper pattern of the jacket made in Step 2, position it carefully on the quilt-top material, and trace the pattern onto the quilt-top. Do not cut it out, however.

19. Set your sewing machine to its largest stitch and stay-stitch 1/16" (.16 cm) outside of the seam lines of the pattern on the material. This will prevent the quilting stitches from coming apart after you cut the material to shape.

20. Cut out the jacket from the pieced fabric.

21. Finish the cuff and lower edges of the jacket with bias binding.

22. Add the collar sash as described in steps 6 through 8 of Apparel Pattern 3 (page 123–124).

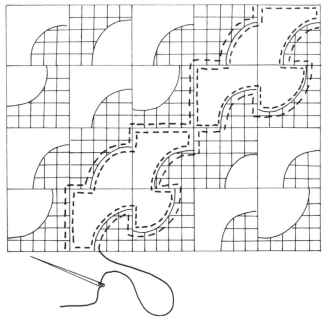

8. Using outline stitching for quilting the Drunkard's Path design.

Honeycomb Quilt Vest

1. Honeycomb Quilt Vest, front and back views.

Octagons and squares comprise the pattern of the Honeycomb Quilt Vest. The combination of geometric shapes produces a complex effect. The octagons lend themselves to scalloped shapes for the edges. The final result is uniquely appealing (see color page F). The versatility of the Honeycomb Quilt is limited only by the quilter's imagination. The pattern pieces are the right front bodice, left front bodice, and back bodice.

Materials

- Dark and light-colored printed cotton fabric or dark and light-colored solid cotton fabric
- Polyester batting: 2 yards (182.8 cm) of 46″ (116.8 cm) wide batting for all pattern sizes
- Backing material: 2 yards (182.8 cm) of 46″ (116.8 cm) wide fabric for all pattern sizes
- Button (optional)
- 6½ yards (594 cm) of bias tape of finished width ½″ (1.3 cm); unfolded width is 2″ (5.1 cm). You may make or purchase the bias tape
- Sewing thread: 1 spool dark; 1 spool light
- Quilting thread: 1 spool dark; 1 spool light
- Basting thread
- Paper
- Template cardboard or plastic
- Apparel Pattern 4: Oversized Vest (page 126)

Directions

1. Enlarge and adjust Apparel Pattern 4, the Oversized Vest. See Chapter 4 for enlarging and adjusting information. Add ⅝″ (1.6 cm) seam allowance to the pattern sections on all sides, except on fold line. Make a second copy of the right bodice front and reverse it for the left bodice front pattern. Set the pattern papers aside.

2. Transfer the patchwork pattern templates to template cardboard or plastic and cut them out. Do not add seam allowances to your templates, to assure uniformity of size.

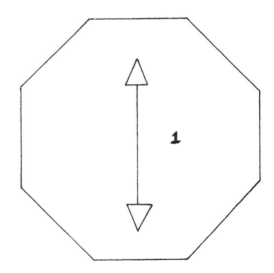

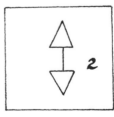

Full-sized templates of the Honeycomb Quilt. Seam allowances are not included. Arrows indicate the straight grain of the fabric.

3. Determine the number of pattern pieces you will need by directly sketching the Honeycomb pattern templates onto your enlarged, adjusted pattern section papers with colored pencils or crayons. Place the right and left bodice front designs symmetrically so that the designs will align across on the finished garment. If you want to scallop the edges of the armholes and bodice hem (as shown in Figure 1 and in the color photo), plan your design so that the outermost octagon shape edge is aligned with the pattern piece sewing lines at the armholes and the bottom of the bodice. Referring to your sketches, count the number of patchwork pieces of each size that you will need for each pattern piece (see Chapter 3 for details of these calculations).

4. Calculate the yardage requirements of your quilt-top (see the section on "Estimating Yardage Requirements" in Chapter 3), and get material.

5. Preshrink all quilt-top fabrics, backing material, and bias tape. Press the fabrics to remove wrinkles.

6. Trace the templates onto your quilt-top fabrics (see "Tracing and Cutting the Quilt-Top Patterns" in Chapter 3). Add ¼" (.6 cm) seam allowances around each piece as you trace it onto your fabric. Trace the number of pieces you need for each color and size, which you calculated in Step 3.

7. Cut the patchwork pieces out one at a time to ensure uniformity.

8. Use your templates to trace and cut out paper patterns of the patchwork pieces, without the seam allowances. You will need as many of these as you have patchwork pieces; if you have cut 200 fabric octagons, you need 200 paper octagon patterns, for example. They will be ¼" (.6 cm) smaller on each side than the fabric octagons.

9. Center a paper octagon pattern on the wrong side of a fabric octagon, as shown in Figure 2. Place a pin in the center to hold the paper pattern onto the fabric patch. Notch the edges of the fabric patch to reduce bulk. Turn the seam allowances toward the wrong side of the fabric, over the paper, and baste them in place (see Figure 3). Repeat this process for all the octagons you need to piece. Do the same with

the square patches. Don't remove the papers when you finish, however.

10. With the wrong side of the quilt-top towards you, join the octagons in a row with whipstitching (see Figure 4). In the model, contrasting thread was used for this, as a decorative element (see color photo). Continue to make rows of octagons; consult your sketches to see how many octagons you need to join for each row.

11. With the wrong side of the quilt-top still towards you, whipstitch the square patches to each row of octagons (Figure 5).

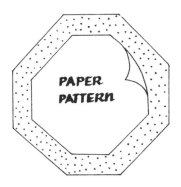

2. Center the paper octagon on the wrong side of the octagonal fabric patch.

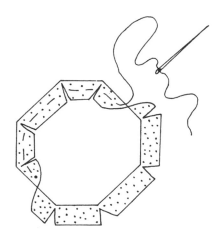

3. Notch and baste the octagonal patches around the paper patterns.

12. Repeat the piecing process given in steps 10 and 11 until you have joined the required number of rows of octagons and squares for each of the three bodice pattern pieces (consult your sketches).

13. After all the patches are whipstitched together, remove the basting stitches around the octagons and squares. This will release the paper patterns from the patches. Iron the quilt-tops to flatten their surfaces.

14. Take the three pieces of quilt-top material you made in Step 10 through 13. For each piece, cut a rectangle of batting and a rectangle of backing. Each rectangle should be 1″ (2.5 cm) larger on each side than your quilt-top pieced material for that apparel pattern section.

15. With one thickness of thread, baste the quilt-top fabric for each bodice piece to the batting and backing rectangles you cut for that bodice piece. See instructions on basting in Chapter 3. Remember to baste away from the center of each pattern piece to smooth out the fabric surface.

16. Quilt each of the basted bodice pieces separately, using outline stitching (see Figure 6). Use light-colored thread for the light-colored patches and dark-colored thread for the dark-colored patches. Remove the basting threads after the quilting is finished.

17. Transfer your enlarged, adjusted apparel patterns to the quilted bodice sections.

18. Set your sewing machine on its largest stitch and stay-stitch 1⁄16″ (.16 cm) outside the seam lines on each bodice piece. This will prevent the quilted fabric from coming apart after you cut the pieces to shape. Follow the shape of the octagons to sew in a scalloped shape along the edges you wish to scallop.

19. Carefully cut out the bodice pieces along the cutting lines. To make the armhole and vest bodice hem in a scalloped pattern, carefully cut the quilt-top material along the octagon edges. Round the corners by snipping off the outer points of the octagon seam allowances in those areas. Pin and baste bias binding to the outside of the pattern pieces in the scalloped areas after the bodice pieces are assembled (see Apparel Pattern 4 for bodice assembly). Stitch the bias binding down on the outside; trim and grade the seam allowances, and notch the bias binding and seam allowances in curved areas. Then turn the bias binding inside and whipstitch it in place on the inside of the vest.

20. Construct the vest according to the directions in Apparel Pattern 4, starting at Step 3. If you wish, make and attach a roulou loop (see Chapter 5), and attach a button to close the vest.

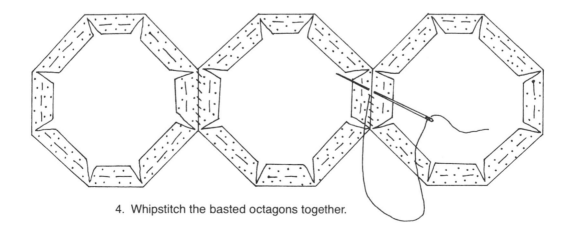

4. Whipstitch the basted octagons together.

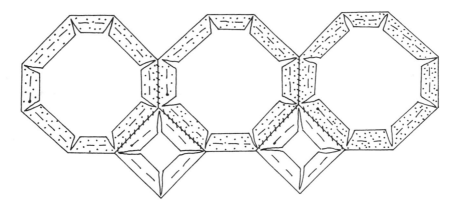

5. Join basted squares to the basted octagons with whipstitching on the back of the quilt-top.

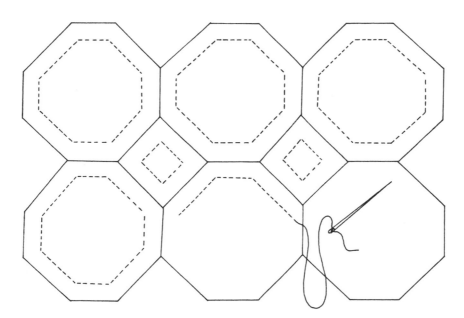

6. Use outline stitching to emphasize the shapes of the patches.

Birds of Paradise Jacket

1. Birds of Paradise Jacket, front and back views.

Five piecing techniques—appliqué, patchwork, reverse appliqué, trapunto, and Seminole piecing—are combined here to create a fantasy garment (see color page A). The jacket uses all 8 pattern pieces of Apparel Pattern 3 (the Kimono Jacket). The bodice does not have an overall layer of batting; loose polyester batting is used for any designs raised with stuffed quilting.

Materials

Note: the colors given below are the colors in the model (see the color photo). Feel free to vary them as you wish.

- Pictorial cotton print fabric (in our model, it has birds and flowers on it)
- Blue cotton fabric for the hemband, collar sash, and Layer 3 of the bodice background (the inner-most layer): about 4 yards (365.8 cm) of 46″ (116.8 cm) wide fabric. Check the amount with your enlarged pattern pieces
- White cotton fabric for Layer 2 of the bodice background (the middle layer): 4 yards (365.8 cm) of 46″ (116.8 cm) wide fabric for all sizes
- Brown cotton fabric for Layer 1 of the bodice background (the topmost layer): 4 yards (365.8 cm) of 46″ (116.8 cm) wide fabric for all sizes
- Piping (optional) for cuff edges and around yoke (black in photo)
- Loose polyester batting, for stuffed design areas; thin bonded polyester batting for hembands, yoke and cuffs
- 4 yards (365.6 cm) of bias tape of finished width ½″ (1.3 cm); unfolded width is 2″ (5.1 cm). You may purchase the bias tape or make it from your fabric.
- Sewing thread: 1 spool dark; 1 spool light
- Quilting thread: 1 spool dark, 1 spool light
- Basting thread
- ¾″ (1.8 cm) wide masking tape
- Template cardboard or plastic
- Apparel Pattern 3: Kimono Jacket (page 119)

Directions

1. Enlarge and adjust the Kimono Jacket Pattern, Apparel Pattern #3. (See Chapter 4 for enlarging and adjusting instructions.)

2. Take the enlarged and adjusted bodice apparel patterns. (The bodice pattern includes the sleeve.) Join the right front bodice and right back bodice patterns at the shoulder seams with adhesive tape (Figure 2). Trace a copy of the joined right bodice pattern and reverse it to be the left front bodice and left back bodice patterns. Join the two halves of the bodice pattern at the center seam to form one single pattern unit for the bodice. Add ⅝″ (1.6 cm) seam allowance around all the edges of the bodice pattern papers.

3. Measure your pattern pieces to estimate how much fabric you will need and get fabric.

4. Preshrink all fabrics, including the bias tape and all layers of the quilt-top material. Press all fabrics to remove wrinkles and set them aside.

5. Using the color photo in the photo section and the sketch (Figure 3) as guides, plan the bodice design you would like and draw it on your bodice pattern paper, using crayons or colored pencils. Plan the position of the decorative parts of your pictorial print fabric and the other design elements of the bodice.

6. Spread the bodice pattern out flat. Cut a rectangle around it with about 1″ (2.5 cm) extra on each side of each of the following: the blue fabric (Layer 3), the white fabric (Layer 2), and the brown fabric (Layer 1). See Figure 3 for guidance. Do not cut the bodice to shape yet, however.

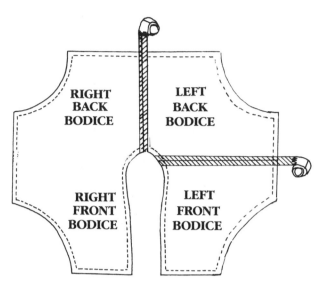

2. Tape the bodice pattern sections together at the shoulder seams and at the center back seam to create one bodice pattern piece.

7. Remove the blue layer and the white layer and set them aside.

8. Referring to your sketches on the bodice pattern papers, cut out the parts you want from your pictorial print fabric. Be sure to leave ¼" (.6 cm) around the final size you want so you have an edge to turn under when you appliqué these pieces to the top layer of the bodice. Trace the bodice pattern shape onto the brown (top) layer, but do not cut it out. Pin the cut-out pieces to the brown layer of the bodice and study the overall effect. Adjust them as necessary.

9. Appliqué the pictorial pieces to the brown layer of the quilt-top. See instructions in Chapter 3 on appliqué techniques. When you finish, iron the fabric.

10. Optional: if you want a raised surface for some of the designs, choose areas to do in trapunto (stuffed quilting). See the section in Chapter 3 on trapunto for information on how to do it.

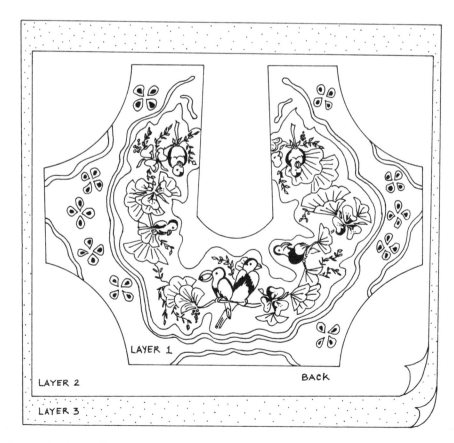

3. Layout for the bodice of the Birds of Paradise Jacket. Top layer (in our model) is brown, Layer 2 is white, and Layer 3 is blue. The printed fabric (birds, etc.) is appliquéd onto the top layer.

11. Baste all three layers of the bodice quilt top together, with the brown on top, the white in the middle, and the blue on the bottom. See instructions on basting in Chapter 3. Remember to baste away from the center of the piece.

12. Draw the petal-shaped template pattern (Figure 4A) onto template cardboard and cut it out. Do not add seam allowances.

13. Study the bodice quilt-top and decide where you want to place the petal motifs. (See the color photo for reference. The petals are blue with white edges in the photo.) Add them to your bodice sketches and modify your sketch if necessary.

14. With masking tape, plot the meandering lines of the bodice by taping directly onto the brown fabric. With pencil or washable pen, trace around the tape to transfer the lines onto the fabric. Make the meandering lines on the bodice with reverse appliqué. On the top layer (brown in our model), draw a line down the center of the ¾″ wide lines you traced around the masking tape. The center line should follow the curves of the lines and be ⅜″ (1 cm) in from the edges of the line. Cut carefully to open up the center line through the top layer of fabric only. This will leave ⅜″ (1 cm) on each side for a seam allowance. Notch and turn under the seam allowance on the top layer, and whipstitch it in place through the middle and bottom layers of the bodice. This will expose the middle layer (white in our model) in the meandering lines. Next, draw a line down the center of the meandering lines on the middle layer, along the length of each line, following the curves of the lines. Cut carefully to open the center line through the middle layer only. This will leave ⅜″ (1 cm) on each side. Notch slightly and turn under about ⅛″ (.3 cm) of the middle layer at the cut edges for a seam allowance. Whipstitch the seam allowance to the bottom layer (see Figure 5). Work with a small section of the design at a time. See Chapter 3 for more information on reverse appliqué.

15. With pencil or washable pen, trace the petal motifs onto the right side of the brown (top) layer of the bodice.

16. Construction of the petals:
    A. Trace the petal template (4A) to the topmost layer (brown fabric). Cut the petal's shape out of the top layer only, being careful not to cut the layers beneath (Figure 4B).
    B. Mark ¼″ (.6 cm) seam allowance around the cut petal's edge. Notch the seam allowance for turning and whipstitch it down through the three layers of fabric (Figure 4C).
    C. Use the petal template to trace a new sewing line on the second layer. Add ¼″ (.6 cm) seam allowance *inside* the sewing line towards the center of the petal (Figure 4D). The line you draw ¼″ in will be the cutting line for the second layer.
    D. On the new cutting line, cut the center petal shape out of the second layer only, as shown in Figure 4E. Be careful not to cut into the third layer (blue in our model).
    E. Notch the seam allowance around the shape you cut in Step D and whipstitch the seam allowance down through the last layer (Figure 4F).
    F. Repeat steps A through E for each petal shape you want to make. When you have finished, set the bodice aside.

17. Take the enlarged, adjusted patterns for the hembands, yoke front, yoke back, and cuffs. Seminole piecing is used to make the quilt-top fabric for these jacket pieces. You can learn more about Seminole piecing in Chapter 3. To make the hembands:
    A. Decide on the width of the fabric strips you want in the finished cuffs and yoke back (see color photo for guidance). Varied widths create interesting effects. Do some pencil sketches on your paper pattern pieces to clarify your ideas.
    B. Cut out the fabric strips for the Seminole piecing of the yoke back and cuffs. Remember to include ¼″ (.6 cm) around each strip for seam allowance when cutting.
    C. With right sides of fabric together, join the strips to make the quilt-top material for the yoke back and cuffs (Figure 6A). Make each as a separate piece of material, which is larger than the pattern piece; follow your pattern sketches for the size and number of strips. Remember that the material must cover the pattern seam allowances as well as the main part of the pattern piece.
    D. For the front yoke and hembands, do a sketch on your paper pattern pieces to see how you would like the design to look. Then make some more strips for Seminole piecing.

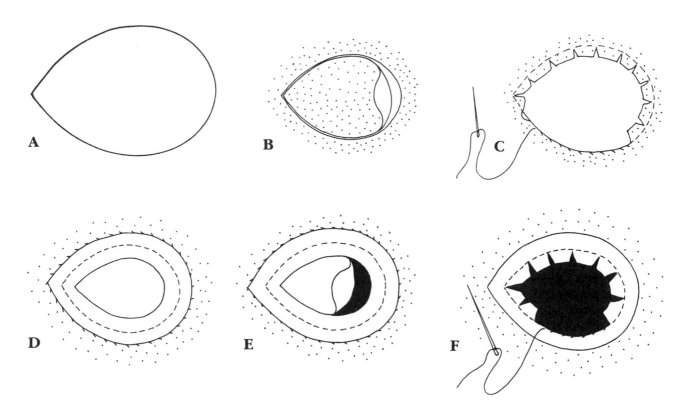

4. A: Petal template, full-sized, without seam allowances.   B: Cut the petal shape out of the top layer (brown).   C: Notch, turn under, and whipstitch the top layer's seam allowance through all 3 layers.   D: For the second layer, a dashed line is traced to make new sewing line. A solid line is drawn ¼″ (.6 cm) inside for the cutting line.   E: Cut the center shape out of the second layer only.   F: Notch, turn under, and whipstitch the seam allowance to the bottom layer.

Cut the sewn strips into bands and stagger them to make the quilt-top material for the front yoke and hembands, as shown in Figure 6B. With right sides of material together, sew the staggered bands together to form the quilt-top material (Figure 6C).

18. Take the pieced quilt-top material you made for the hembands, cuffs, and front and back yokes. Cut the backing and batting material for each of these sections in rectangles that are 1″ (2.5 cm) larger in each dimension than the quilt-top material. Do not cut the quilt-top material to shape yet, however.

19. For each of the hemband sections and cuff sections, and the front and back yokes, baste the three layers of quilt-top, batting, and backing together. (See Chapter 3 for information on basting.)

20. Quilt each piece you basted in Step 19 with outline stitching.

21. Take the apparel pattern of your bodice, position it on the bodice quilt-top material you decorated earlier, and trace the pattern of the bodice onto your quilt-top material.

22. Take the apparel patterns of the hembands, yokes, and cuffs, position each pattern on the quilt-top material you pieced for the respective sections, and trace the apparel pattern onto the pieced material. Do not cut out the fabric yet, however.

23. Set your sewing machine to its largest stitch and stay-stitch ¹⁄₁₆″ (.16 cm) outside of the seam lines on each bodice piece, and also outside the seam lines of each of the cuff, hemband, and yoke pieces. This will prevent the quilting

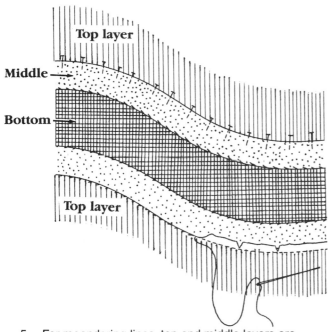

5. For meandering lines, top and middle layers are cut, pinned and appliquéd in place with whipstitching (reverse appliqué).

stitches from coming apart after you cut the pieces to shape.

24. Carefully cut out the bodice from the decorated fabric you completed in Step 16.

25. Carefully cut out the hembands, yokes, and cuffs from their respective pieced quilt-tops.

26. Cut out the collar sash from solid blue material.

27. Construct the jacket according to the directions in Apparel Pattern 3 (Kimono Jacket), starting at Step 3.

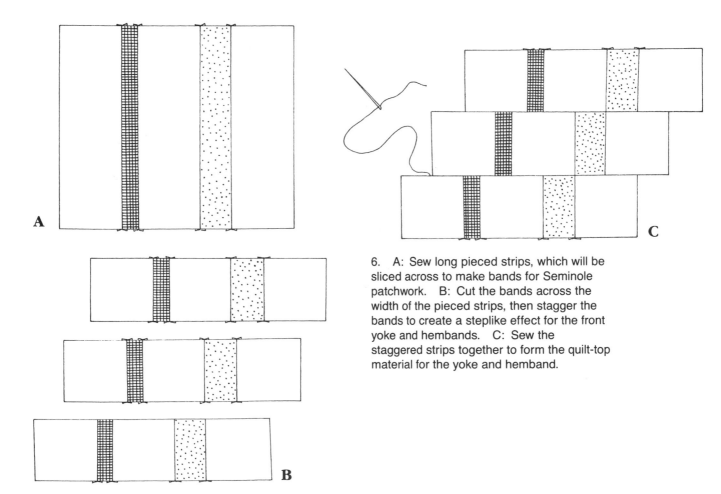

6. A: Sew long pieced strips, which will be sliced across to make bands for Seminole patchwork. B: Cut the bands across the width of the pieced strips, then stagger the bands to create a steplike effect for the front yoke and hembands. C: Sew the staggered strips together to form the quilt-top material for the yoke and hemband.

PROJECT 13

Octagon Star Jacket

1. Octagon Star Jacket, front and back views.

The Octagon Star is a dynamic pattern whose interest lies in the starburst pattern of the printed fabrics against the light background fabric (see color page H). The diamonds that make up the background can also be viewed as a floral motif. The kaleidoscopic effect is as enjoyable today as it was in heirloom quilts of old.

Materials

- Scraps of printed cotton fabric
- Light, solid-colored cotton fabric
- Dark, solid-colored cotton fabric for collar sash, hemband and cuffs
- Backing material: 4 yards (365.8 cm) of 46" (116.8 cm) wide fabric for all sizes of apparel pattern
- 4 yards (365.8 cm) of bias tape of finished width ½" (1.3 cm); unfolded width is 2" (5.1 cm), made from the same solid-colored fabric used for the collar sash, hembands, and cuffs (tape is used for finishing inside jacket seams)
- Polyester batting: 4 yards (365.8 cm) of 46" (116.8 cm) wide batting for all sizes of apparel pattern
- Sewing thread: light and dark colors to match the quilt-top fabrics
- Quilting thread: light and dark colors to match the quilt-top fabrics
- Basting thread
- Template cardboard or plastic
- 3 Frogs to close jacket (optional; see color photo)
- Apparel Pattern 3: Kimono Jacket (page 119)

Directions

1. Take the Kimono Jacket pattern on page 120. Trace out the entire page as one pattern piece, including the right front and back bodice sections and the front and back yokes. Lengthen the yoke and bodice pattern front and back each

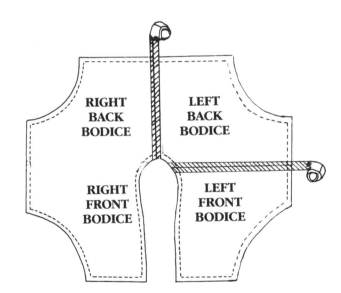

2. Tape the bodice pattern sections together to make 1 bodice pattern piece.

by 4". Then enlarge and adjust the pattern. (See Chapter 4 for enlarging and adjusting instructions.)

2. Trace a copy of the right jacket pattern made in Step 1 and reverse it for the left jacket pattern. Tape the right and left patterns together to create a single main pattern piece (Figure 2). Add ⅝" (1.6 cm) seam allowance around all the edges of the bodice pattern.

3. Transfer the patchwork pattern templates to template material and cut them out. Do not add seam allowances to your templates, to assure uniformity of size. Also make a template of the block for the Octagon Star, Figure 3. It will be a help in your next step.

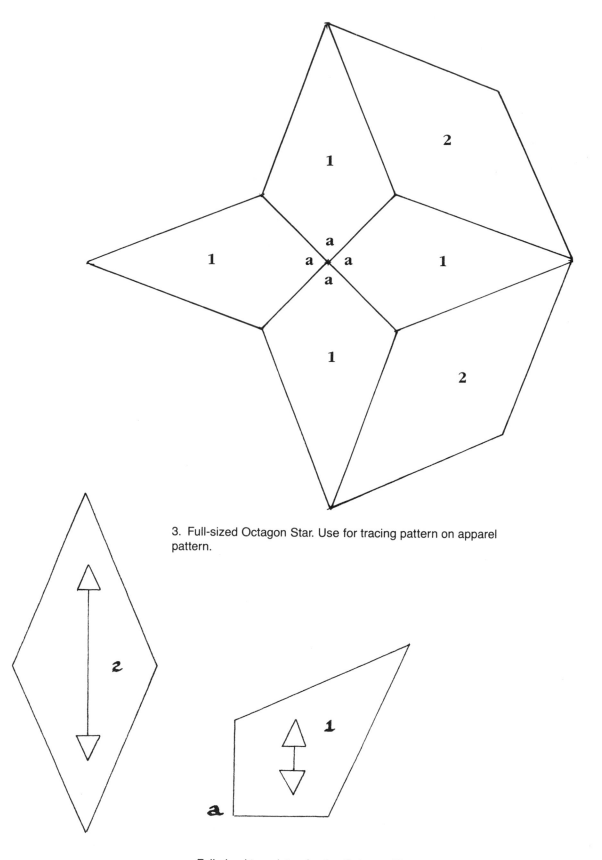

3. Full-sized Octagon Star. Use for tracing pattern on apparel pattern.

Full-sized templates for the Octagon Star.

4. Determine the number of blocks you will need by directly sketching the Octagon Star blocks onto your enlarged, adjusted jacket pattern paper, using colored pencils or crayons. Place the right and left jacket front designs symmetrically so that the designs will align across on the finished garment. Multiply the total number of blocks you need by the number of pieces of each size and color in each block, to estimate the total number of patchwork pieces you will need to cut of each size and color (see Chapter 3 for details of these calculations).

5. Calculate the yardage requirements of your quilt-top (see the section on "Estimating Yardage Requirements" in Chapter 3), and get material.

6. Preshrink all quilt-top fabrics, backing material, and bias tape. Press the fabrics to remove wrinkles.

7. Trace the templates onto your quilt-top fabrics (see "Tracing and Cutting the Quilt-Top Patterns" in Chapter 3). Add ¼" (.6 cm) seam allowances around each piece as you trace it onto your fabric. Trace the number of pieces you need for each color and size, which you calculated in Step 4.

8. Cut the patchwork pieces out one at a time to ensure uniformity.

9. Cut out a paper pattern piece for each fabric patchwork piece. If you need 400 of Piece 2, you will need to cut 400 paper patterns, for example. The paper pattern pieces should be traced from the templates. Cut them out without adding seam allowances.

10. Center a paper pattern on the wrong side of a fabric patch, as shown in Figure 4. Place a pin in the center to hold the paper pattern onto the fabric patch. Notch the edges of the fabric patch to reduce bulk. Turn the seam allowances toward the wrong side of the fabric, over the paper, and baste them in place (see Figure 4). Repeat this process for all the patchwork pieces you need for the jacket quilt-top, for both sizes of pieces. Don't remove the papers when you finish, however.

11. With the wrong side of the pieces facing towards you, join four basted Piece 1 shapes in a star with whipstitching (see Figure 5). Repeat this to make as many star-shapes from the Piece-1 shapes as you need for the quilt-top. Do

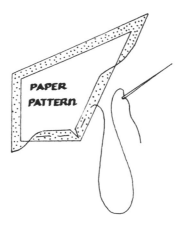

4. Insert paper pattern and turn seam allowances to wrong side; notch them and baste them in place.

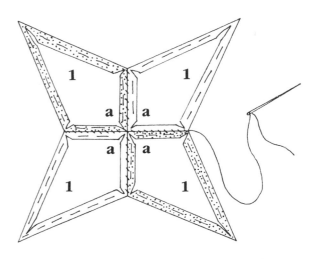

5. Join 4 of Shape 1 in the center with whipstitching from the wrong side to make a star.

not remove the paper patterns yet, however.

12. With the wrong side of the pieced material facing you, use whipstitching to join Piece 2 between the star units you made in Step 10 (see Figure 6). Consult your pattern sketches to see how many of the octagon patterns you need to join for each row, and continue the piecing until the desired width of each row is made. Attach the Piece 2 shapes below the rows of star shapes as shown in Figure 6. Join the rows to make the quilt-top.

13. Remove the basting, which will release the paper patterns from the quilt-top.

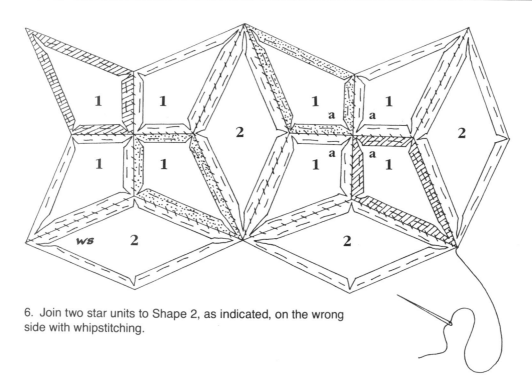

6. Join two star units to Shape 2, as indicated, on the wrong side with whipstitching.

14. After you have pieced the entire quilt-top, cut the batting and backing material in a rectangle that is 1″ (2.5 cm) larger on each side than the pieced material.

15. Baste the quilt-top, batting, and binding layers together (see basting instructions in Chapter 3).

16. Quilt the layers with outline stitching. Use light-colored thread for the light background sections and dark-colored thread for the dark background sections.

17. Remove the basting stitches after quilting.

18. Take the paper pattern made in Step 2, position it carefully on the quilt-top material, and trace the pattern onto the quilt top. Do not cut out the shape yet, however.

19. Set your sewing machine to its largest stitch and stay-stitch ⅛″ (.3 cm) outside of the seam lines of the bodice. This will prevent the quilting stitches from coming apart after you cut the bodice to shape.

20. Cut out the pattern carefully from the pieced fabric.

21. Protect the inner seams under the arms by finishing them with bias binding.

22. Seam the jacket front to the back from the sleeve edge to the bottom of the bodice.

23. Construct the cuffs and collar sash according to the directions in Apparel Pattern 3, steps 5 through 8. The collar sash should extend 2⅝″ below the end of the jacket front.

24. Measure the bottom of the jacket all around, from the front opening, around the back, and to the front again. Cut a length of fabric of the same width (3¼″ or 8.2 cm) and material as the collar sash, for a finishing hemband at the bottom of the jacket. The length should be what you measured around the bottom plus ⅝″ seam allowance on each side.

25. With right sides of material facing in, fold the hemband lengthwise and sew across the seam line of each short end to close the short sides. Attach one long side of the hemband to the outside of the jacket bottom along the seam line, with right sides of material facing. Turn one half of the width of the hemband inside and whipstitch the seam allowance to the inside of the jacket bottom and to the collar sash ends.

26. Add frogs to close jacket, if you wish.

Basic Vest

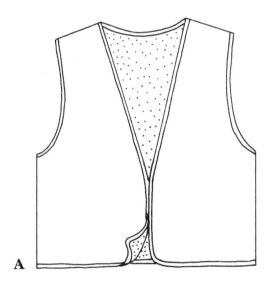

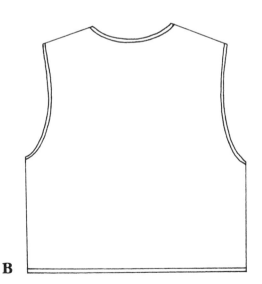

1. Basic Vest (Apparel Pattern 1).
A: Front view.   B: back view.

The Basic Vest has two pattern pieces: the right front bodice (Figure 2), which is reversed for the left front bodice, and the back bodice (Figure 3).

Directions

1. Enlarge and adjust the apparel patterns for the right front bodice and the back bodice (figures 2 and 3). Add ⅝″ (1.6 cm) seam allowance around them. Reverse the right front bodice

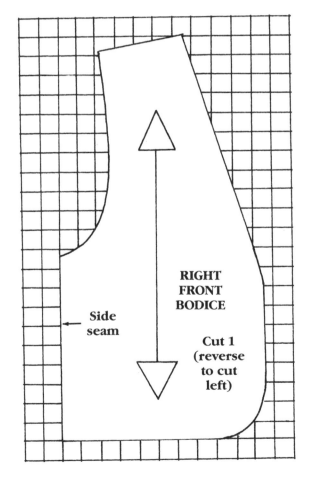

RIGHT FRONT BODICE

← Side seam

Cut 1 (reverse to cut left)

2. Pattern for right front bodice of the Basic Vest. Reverse the pattern for the left front bodice. Size, medium. Scale: 1 box = 1 in.² (2.5 cm × 2.5 cm).

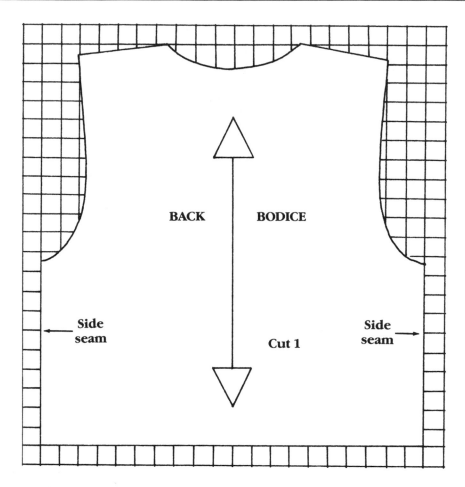

3. Pattern for back bodice of the Basic Vest. Size, medium. Scale: 1 box = 1 in.² (2.5 cm × 2.5 cm).

pattern to cut the left front bodice pattern. Carefully transfer the patterns to your pieced (patchwork), quilted material, being sure to match the patterns for the bodice fronts so that the two halves are symmetrically placed. Stay-stitch and cut out the bodice parts from the pieced material.

2. With right sides of fabric facing, sew the front bodice sections to the back bodice section at the shoulder seams and side seams (Figure 4).

3. Trim the sewn seam allowances to ½" (1.3 cm) and finish them with a zigzag or overlock stitch (see Chapter 5).

4. If you decide to make vest closures, there are several kinds possible, including ties made of bias binding, roulou loops and buttons, or frogs; see Chapter 5 for instructions.

5. Finish the raw edges of the vest with bias binding, as described in Chapter 5. Iron the vest after construction.

4. Sewing the front bodice pieces to the back bodice at the shoulders and the side seams.

Asymmetrical Vest

The Asymmetrical Vest has two pattern pieces: the front bodice and the back bodice (Figure 2).

Directions

1. Enlarge and adjust the patterns (Figure 2). (See Chapter 4 regarding enlarging and adjusting.) Add ⅝″ (1.6 cm) seam allowance around them. Carefully pin the patterns to your pieced (patchwork), quilted material and cut out the front and back bodice.

2. With the right sides of the material facing, sew the front bodice to the back bodice at the right shoulder seam and the side seams (Figure 3). Iron the seams open.

3. Make two or three roulou loops out of solid-colored material (see Chapter 5). Attach the roulou loops to the left shoulder part of the front bodice.

4. Finish the raw edges of the vest with bias binding (see Chapter 5). Iron the vest flat after construction.

5. Sew shanked buttons to the left shoulder of the back bodice of the vest, so that they fit comfortably in the roulou loops.

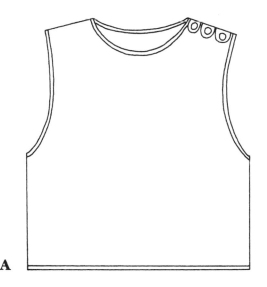

A

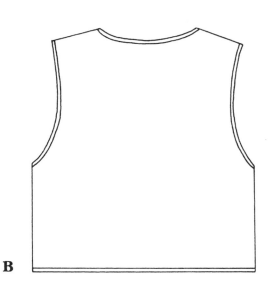

B

1. Asymmetrical Vest (Apparel Pattern 2).
A: Front view.   B: Back view.

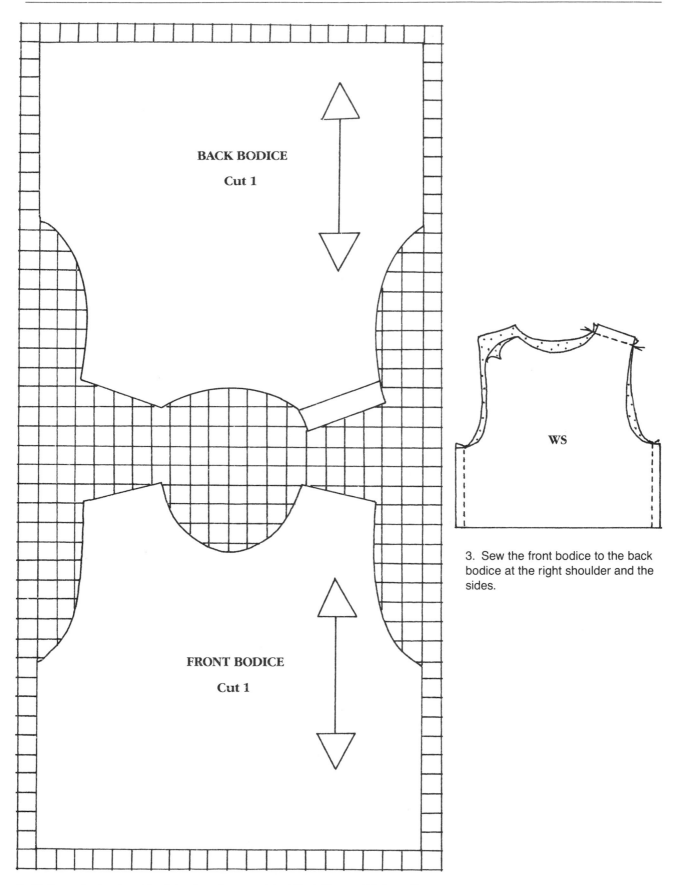

BACK BODICE

Cut 1

FRONT BODICE

Cut 1

WS

3. Sew the front bodice to the back bodice at the right shoulder and the sides.

2. Patterns for front and back bodice, Asymmetrical Vest (Apparel Pattern 2); size, medium. Scale: 1 box = 1 in.² (2.5 cm × 2.5 cm).

Kimono Jacket

The Kimono Jacket pattern has 8 pattern pieces. The right front bodice, right back bodice, right front yoke, and back yoke are given in Figure 3. The front hemband, back hemband, and cuff are in Figure 4. The collar sash is in Figure 5. The number of pieces to cut is indicated on each. If you have enough material, you can enlarge and cut the front and back bodice pieces as one piece. The right bodice patterns and right front yoke pattern should be reversed to make the left bodice patterns and the left front yoke.

Enlarge, adjust, and cut out your paper patterns (see Chapter 4). Follow the design (quilt-top) piecing instructions for the particular design that you have chosen. Cut the rest of the pieces out of material as you need them, checking each paper pattern piece against the assembled garment and adjusting it as necessary before you cut your material. Directions for assembling the Kimono Jacket are given below.

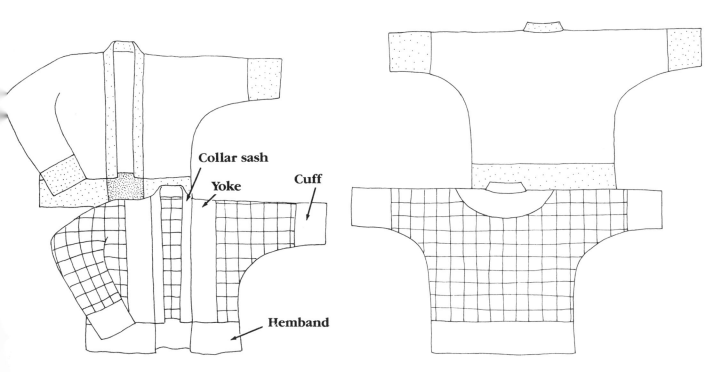

1. Front views of Apparel Pattern 3, the Kimono Jacket, with the yoke (below) and without (above).

2. Back view of Apparel Pattern 3, Kimono Jacket, with the yoke (below) and without (above).

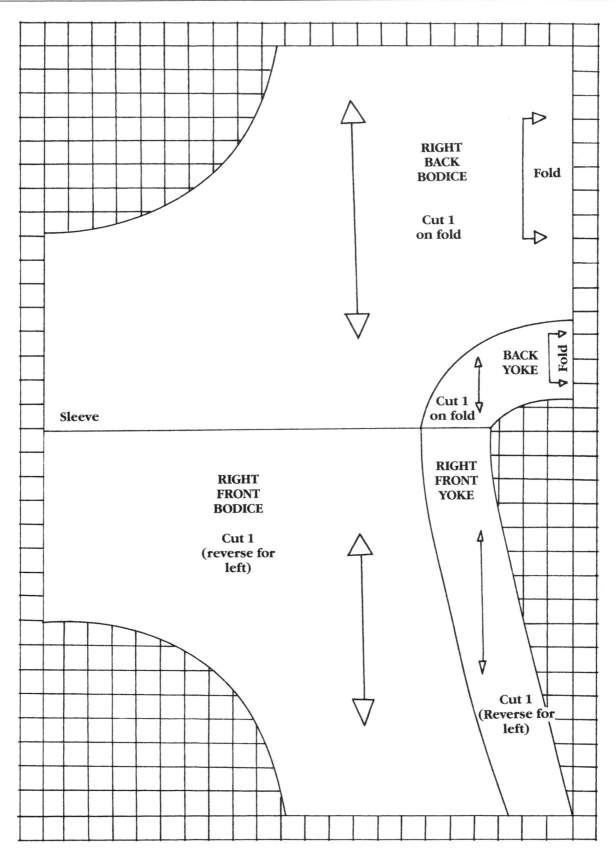

3. Right front and right back bodice patterns for Apparel Pattern 3, the Kimono Jacket; right front yoke pattern; back yoke pattern. (Bodice pattern includes sleeve.) Scale: one box = 1 in.² (2.5 cm × 2.5 cm). Reverse the patterns to get the left front and left back bodice patterns and the left back yoke pattern.

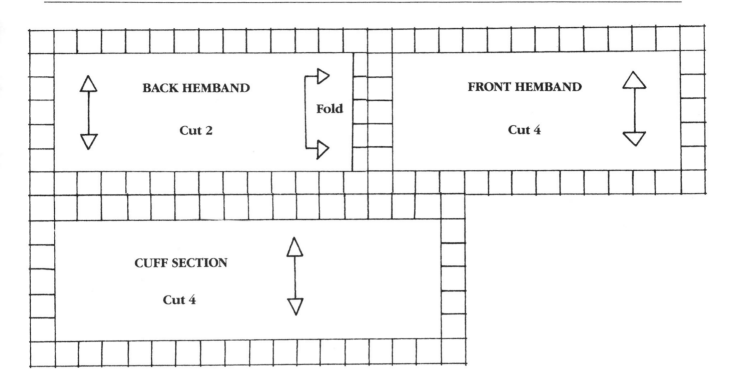

4. Hemband and cuff patterns for Apparel Pattern 3, Kimono Jacket. Scale: one box = 1 in.² (2.5 cm × 2.5 cm).

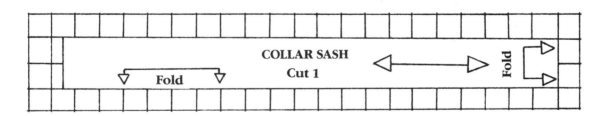

5. Collar sash pattern for Apparel Pattern 3, Kimono Jacket. Scale: one box = 1 in.² (2.5 cm × 2.5 cm).

Directions

Unless noted, all construction is done with right sides of material facing each other.

1. Sew the front bodice sections to the back bodice at the shoulder seams (Figure 6). Press the seams open.

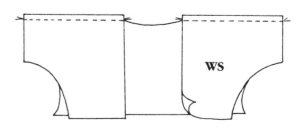

6. Sew the front bodice sections to the back bodice at the shoulder seams.

2. Sew the front bodice sections to the back bodice at the side seams (Figure 7). Press the seams open.

3. Sew the front yoke sections to the back yoke on a short side (Figure 8). Press the seams open.

4. Pin the yokes around the bodice sections, as shown (Figure 9), and sew. Press the seams open.

5. Take the four cuff sections and form the cuffs of the jacket as follows:

  A. Take one cuff section and sew its short seams together, as shown in Figure 10. Repeat this for the remaining 3 cuff sections. Press the seams open.

  B. With the right sides of the material facing, slip one cuff section inside the other, aligning seams. Stitch around the cuff sections at one seam line to form the cuff (see Figure 11). Repeat this to make the second cuff.

  C. Trim the seam allowance of the edge you just sewed to ½″ (1.3 cm) to reduce bulk. You may reduce the seam allowance to less than ½″ if the fabric is very bulky.

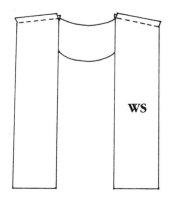

8. Sew the front and back yoke sections together.

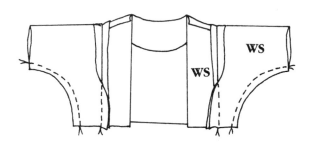

9. Sew the yokes to the bodice.

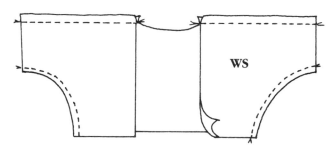

7. Sew the front bodice sections to the back bodice at the side seams.

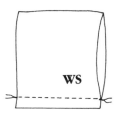

10. Sew each cuff section as shown.

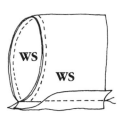

11. With right sides of material facing, slip one cuff section inside the other, aligning seams, and stitch around it on one side on the seam line.

D. Open out the cuff section and turn the right side of the material in, as shown in Figure 12A. With right sides of material facing, pin the cuff on the outside of the jacket sleeve as shown, matching seam lines and raw edges, and sew around the sleeve opening to attach the cuff unit. Repeat this process for the second sleeve and cuff. Grade and notch seam allowances to reduce bulk.

E. Turn the garment wrong-side out. Turn one section of the cuff to the inside as shown in Figure 13, turn the seam allowance under, and whipstitch it in place.

6. Fold the collar sash along its length and sew the short edges as shown in Figure 14. Grade the sewn seams to reduce bulk, turn the sash right-side out, and press it.

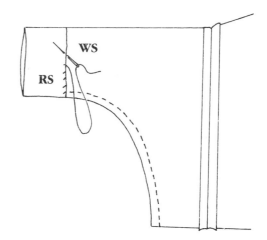

13. Turn the bodice to the wrong side, turn the unattached cuff unit inside, and turn in the seam allowance. Whipstitch the cuff in place as shown.

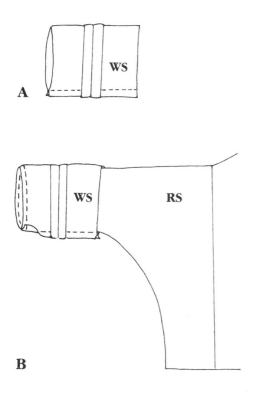

12.   A: Cuff unit opened up, with right side of material turned in.   B: With the cuff unit unfolded and facing right-side in, pin it to the outside of the jacket sleeve, with raw edges and seam lines matching. Sew around the sleeve opening on the seam line to attach cuff unit.

14. Fold collar sash on its length and seam the short sides to themselves.

7. With the right side of the collar-sash material facing the right side of the yoke (Figure 15), pin one thickness of the collar sash to the outside of the yoke, aligning raw edges. Stitch the collar sash to the yoke all around. Then trim the seam allowance to ½″ (1.3 cm) to reduce bulk. Notch around the curved areas. Press the collar sash flat toward the center of the garment so that the outside of the collar sash and the jacket form a flat surface.

8. On the inside of the jacket bodice, turn under the seam allowance of the long, raw edge of the collar sash and pin it in place. Whipstitch it to the inside of the yoke (Figure 16) and press it.

9. Take one back hemband and two front hemband sections. Sew them together on their short sides to form one hemband unit (Figure 17). Repeat this process to make a second hemband unit.

10. Sew the two hemband units together on both short ends and on one long side (Figure 18). Reduce the sewn seam allowances to ½″ (1.3 cm), and press.

11. Pin one raw edge of the hemband to the outside of the jacket bodice with right sides of material facing, matching front openings and raw edges of seam allowances. Sew the pinned edge of the hemband to the jacket bodice at the bottom seam line, as shown in Figure 19. Trim the seam allowances to ½″.

12. Press the hem unit down, flat with the top of the jacket. Turn one hem section to the inside of the jacket bodice, as shown in Figure 20. Turn the seam allowance in, pin the hemband in place, and whipstitch it down to the jacket bodice.

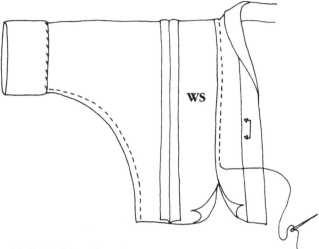

15. With right sides of material facing, stitch the collar sash to the yoke all around the jacket opening.

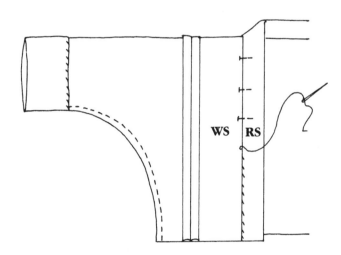

16. After turning under the seam allowance, whipstitch the collar sash to the inside of the yoke and press it.

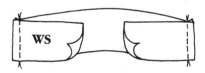

17. Seam two front hemband sections to the back hemband on the short sides.

18. Seam two hemband units together along one long side and both short sides.

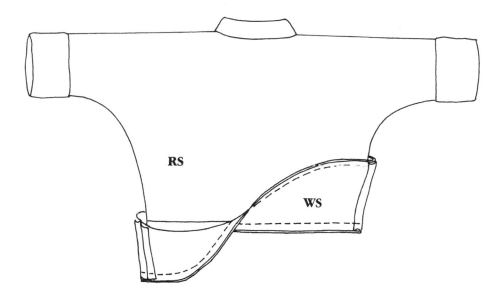

19. Pin the raw edge of a hemband unit to the raw edge at the bottom of the bodice on the outside of the bodice, with right sides of material facing. Sew along bottom of bodice at seam line, all around the bodice.

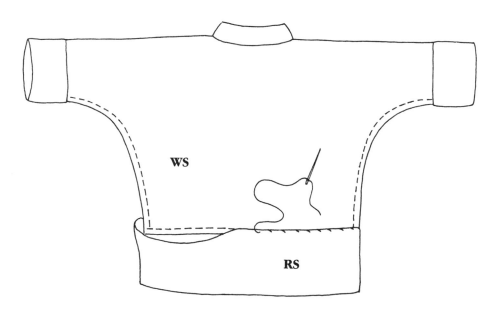

20. Turn one hemband unit inside, turn its seam allowance in, and whipstitch it in place.

Oversized Vest

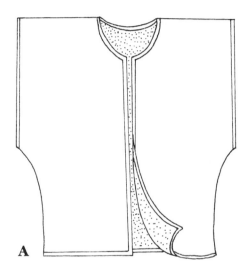

The two pattern pieces for the Oversized Vest are shown in figures 2 and 3. In these figures, three pattern sizes are offered: small (the innermost line), medium (the middle line), and large (the outermost line).

Directions

1. Choose the pattern of the size that seems most appropriate and enlarge it; then adjust it (see Chapter 4). Add ⅝″ (1.6 cm) seam allowances on all sides except where there is a fold line. Reverse the right front bodice pattern for the left front bodice.

2. Carefully transfer the patterns to your pieced, quilted (patchwork) material, being sure to match the patterns for the bodice fronts so that the two halves are symmetrically placed. Stay-stitch and cut out the bodice parts from the pieced material.

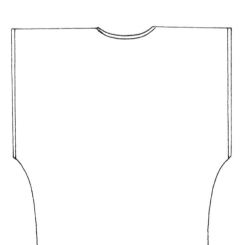

1. Oversized Vest, Apparel Pattern 4.
A: Front view. B: back view.

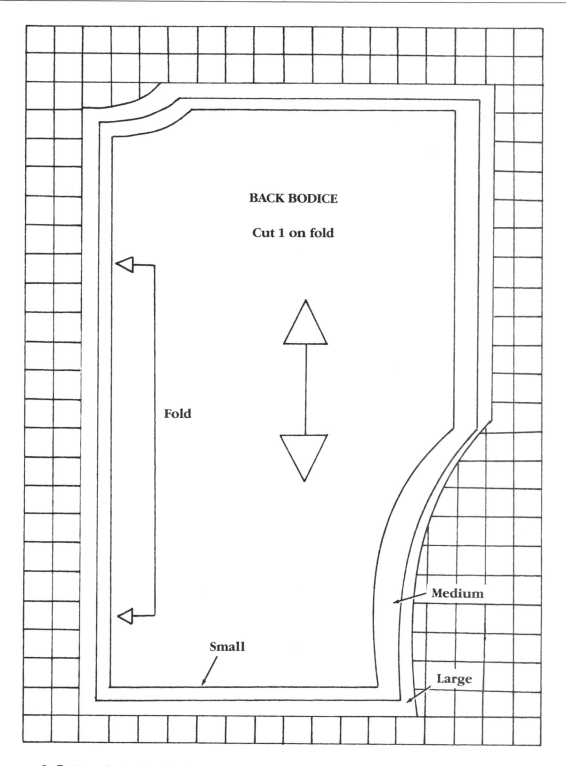

BACK BODICE

Cut 1 on fold

Fold

Small

Medium

Large

2. Patterns for the back bodice, Oversized Vest, in three sizes: small (inner line); medium (middle line); and large (outermost line). Scale: 1 box = 1 in.² (2.5 cm × 2.5 cm). Choose the appropriate one and enlarge it.

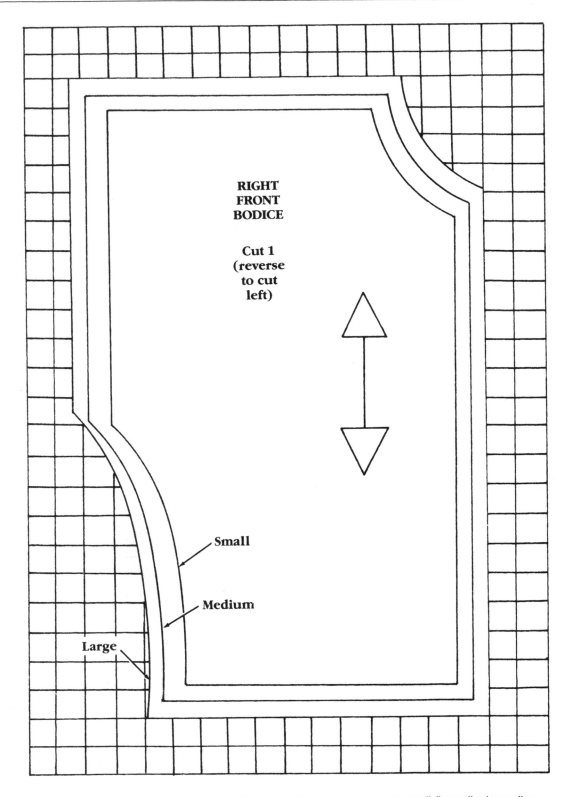

3. Patterns for the right front bodice, Oversized Vest, in three sizes: small (inner line); medium (middle line); and large (outermost line). Scale: 1 box = 1 in.² (2.5 cm × 2.5 cm). Choose the appropriate one and enlarge it.

3. With right sides of material facing, sew the back to the front of the vest at the shoulders and sides (Figure 4).

4. Notch the curved areas of the seam allowances, trim the seam allowances, and finish them with a zigzag or overlock stitch (see Chapter 5).

5. If you decide to make vest closures, there are several kinds possible, including ties made of bias binding, roulou loops and buttons, or frogs; see Chapter 5 for instructions.

6. Finish the raw edges of the vest with bias binding, as described in Chapter 5. Iron the vest after construction.

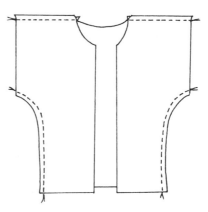

4. With right sides of material facing, seam the bodice front pieces to the bodice back at the shoulders and sides.

Tailored Jacket

The Tailored Jacket has 5 pattern pieces: the right front bodice, the bodice back, the cuff, the sleeve, and the collar (figures 2 and 3). The right front bodice pattern is reversed to cut the left front bodice.

Directions

Unless otherwise noted, all construction is done with right sides of material facing each other.

1. Enlarge and adjust the apparel pattern pieces (see Chapter 4 regarding enlarging and adjusting patterns). Add ⅝″ (1.6 cm) seam allowance around them, except on sides that represent a fold. Carefully transfer the bodice front and back patterns to your pieced (patchwork), quilted material, being sure to match the patterns for the bodice fronts so that the front pieces are placed symmetrically on the pattern. Stay-stitch and cut out the bodice front and back from the pieced material.

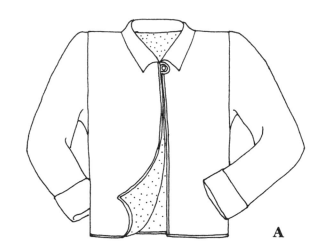

A

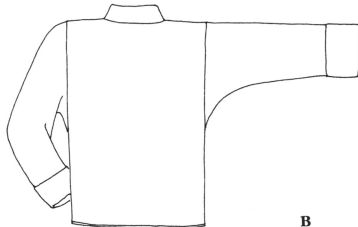

B

1. Tailored Jacket (Apparel Pattern 5).   A: Front view.
B: back view.

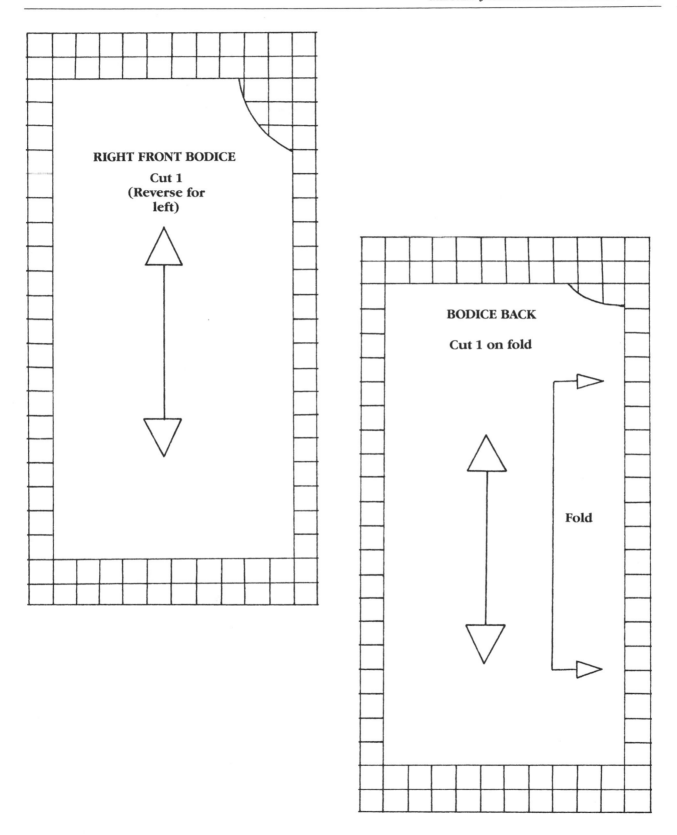

2. Front and back bodice patterns for the Tailored Jacket (Apparel Pattern 5). Size, one size. Scale: 1 box = 1 in.² (2.5 cm × 2.5 cm).

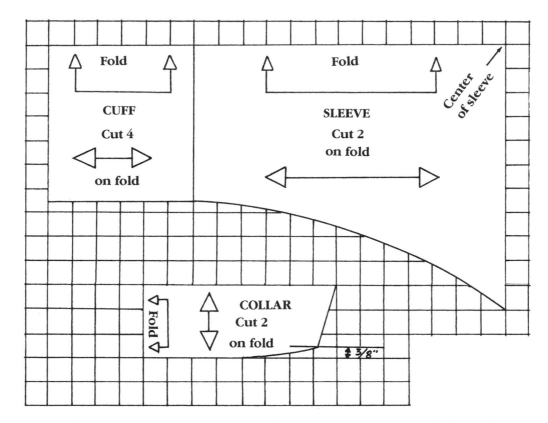

3. Cuff, sleeve, and collar patterns for the Tailored Jacket (Apparel Pattern 5). Scale: 1 box = 1 in.² (2.5 cm × 2.5 cm).

2. Attach the front bodice sections to the back bodice at the shoulders (Figure 4). Then attach a sleeve to each side of the jacket bodice, as shown in Figure 4, matching the center of the sleeve with the seam connecting the front and back bodices.

3. Fold the jacket as shown in Figure 5, pin the sleeve side seams and the jacket front to the jacket back at the sides, and sew the seams as indicated in Figure 5, from the end of the sleeve to the jacket hem.

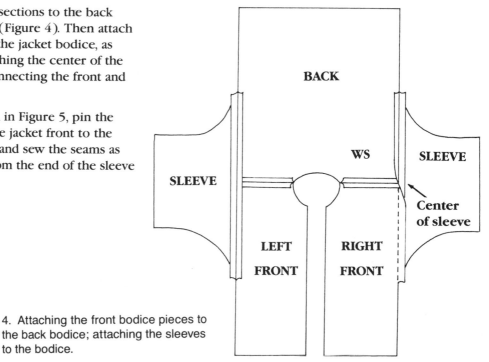

4. Attaching the front bodice pieces to the back bodice; attaching the sleeves to the bodice.

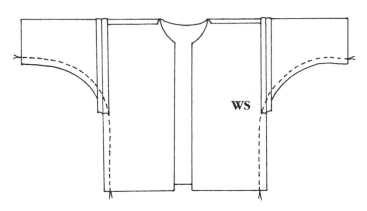

5. Sewing the side seams of the bodice and sleeves.

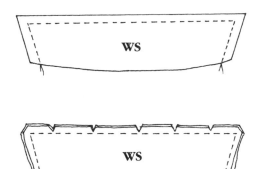

7. Making the collar. A: sewing the seams. B: notching and grading the seams.

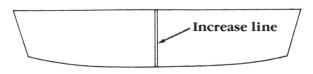

6. Collar, showing line at which the length of collar can be decreased or increased.

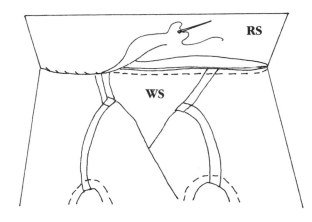

8. Whipstitching the top of the collar to the inside of the jacket. The seam allowance is turned in.

4. Measure the collar pattern against the jacket. If the collar needs to be increased, increase the collar along the increase line (see Figure 6), and cut out a collar of the correct size.

5. Sew and grade the collar, by trimming away one seam allowance slightly more than the other, after the collar seams are sewn (Figure 7). Notch the seam allowance and trim it at the collar points to remove bulk (Figure 7B).

6. Turn the collar right-side out and iron it. Leaving the top side of the collar free, pin and sew the lower layer of the collar to the outside of the jacket bodice. Reduce the seam allowance to ½″ (1.3 cm) after it is sewn.

7. Attach the raw edge of the top side of the collar to the inside of the jacket bodice with whipstitching, as shown in Figure 8, after turning under the seam allowance.

8. Take the four cuff sections and sew each cuff section as shown. (Figure 9).

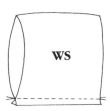

9. Sew each cuff section as shown.

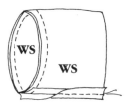

10. With right sides of material facing, slip one cuff section inside the other, aligning seams, and stitch around it on one side.

9. With right sides of material facing, slip one cuff section inside the other, aligning seams, and stitch around it (Figure 10).

10. Open the cuff unit up and with material turned right-side in, pin it to the outside of the jacket sleeve, with raw edges and seam lines matching. Sew around the sleeve opening to attach the cuff unit (Figure 11).

11. Turn the bodice to wrong-side out, turn the unattached cuff unit inside the jacket, and turn in the seam allowance. Whipstitch it in place as shown (Figure 12).

12. If you wish to keep the jacket closed, make and attach a roulou loop and button, as shown in Figure 1A. Finish the remaining raw edges with bias binding. (See Chapter 5 on making and attaching roulou loops and bias binding.)

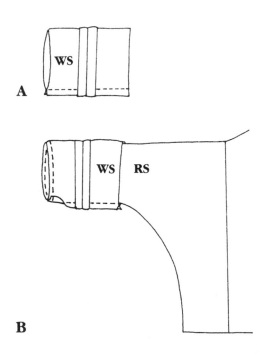

11. A: Cuff unit opened up, with right side of material turned in. B: With the cuff unit unfolded, but facing right-side in, pin it to the outside of the jacket sleeve, with raw edges and seam lines matching. Sew around the sleeve opening to attach cuff unit.

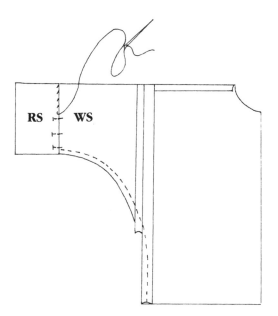

12. Turn the bodice to the wrong side, turn the unattached cuff unit inside, and turn in the seam allowance. Whipstitch it in place as shown.

Mosaic

The octagon shape that is the main design element in Mosaic shows up well when the triangles and squares that form the octagon are close to each other in darkness of color and vary from the pieces around them.

Directions

Trace the template patterns onto template cardboard or plastic and cut out the templates. Do not add seam allowances to the templates. As you trace around the templates on your fabric, add ¼" (.6 cm) seam allowance around each piece. Cut out the pieces from the fabric.

All piecing is done with right sides of material facing and with seam allowances of ¼" (.6 cm). Press seam allowances open after each new piece is added.

1. The Mosaic Quilt-Top.

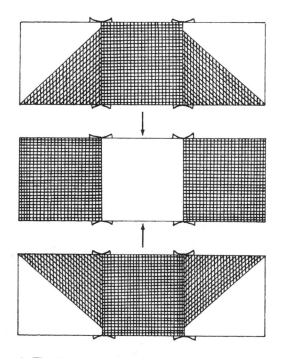

2. Full-sized Mosaic Block, without seam allowances. Size: 4″ × 4″ (10.2 cm × 10.2 cm).

In our sketch (Figure 1) pattern pieces 5–8 have varying colors and designs. To piece a Mosaic Block (Figure 2):

1. Join Triangle 1 to Triangle 2 on their long sides, forming a pieced square (Figure 3). Make 3 more pieced squares in the same way.

2. Form the top row of the octagon block by sewing a Square 3 between the two pieced squares you made in Step 1. Make the bottom row in the same way (see Figure 4). Set them aside.

3. Sew three squares together to form the middle strip of the octagon block (see Figure 4, middle).

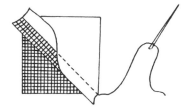

3. Join Triangle 1 to Triangle 2 to make a pieced square.

4. The three rows that form the octagon block.

4. Join the three rows you made in steps 2 and 3, to form the octagon block (see Figure 5).

5. Join square 5, 6, and 7 to form a fourth row that goes below the octagon block (see Figure 2); then join the row to the bottom of the octagon block (Figure 6).

6. Make a strip of square 5, 6, 7, and 8 (see Figure 2) and sew them to the octagon block to complete the Mosaic Block (Figure 7).

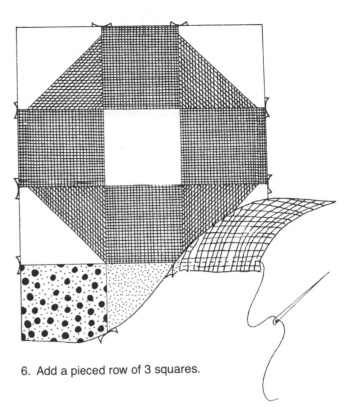

6. Add a pieced row of 3 squares.

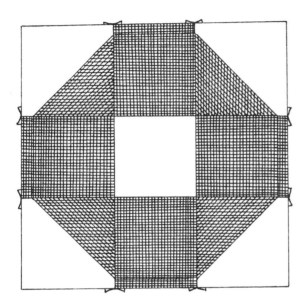

5. The three rows joined to form the octagon block.

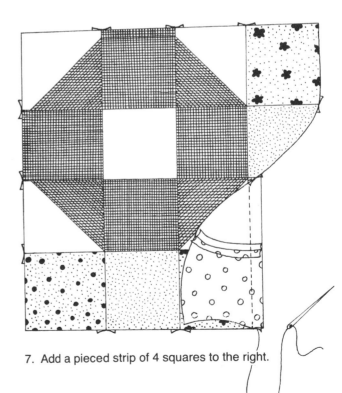

7. Add a pieced strip of 4 squares to the right.

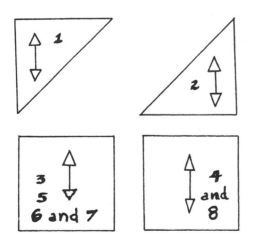

Full-sized templates for the Mosaic Block. Seam allowances are not included. Arrows indicate straight grain of fabric.

Butterflies

1. The Butterflies quilt-top.

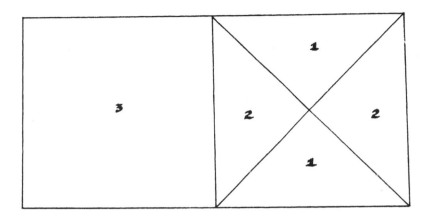

2. Full-sized Butterflies Block (at right) attached to solid square. Butterflies Block measures 2″ × 2″ (5.1 cm × 5.1 cm) without seam allowances.

Directions

Trace the template patterns onto template cardboard or plastic and cut out the templates. Do not add seam allowances to the templates. As you trace around the templates on your fabric, add ¼″ (.6 cm) seam allowance around each piece. Cut out the pieces from the fabric.

All piecing is done with right sides of material facing and with seam allowances of ¼″ (.6 cm). Press seam allowances open after each new piece is added.

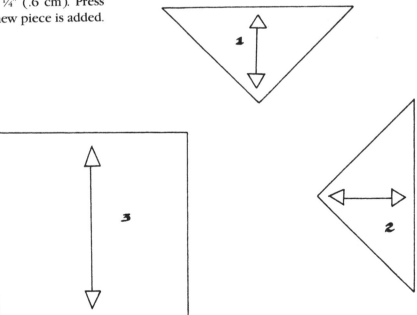

Full-sized templates for the Butterflies Block and solid square. Seam allowances are not included. Arrows indicate straight grain of fabric.

To piece a Butterflies Block (Figure 2):

1. Sew Triangle 1 to Triangle 2 on their short sides to make a large pieced square. Make another in the same way (Figure 3).

2. Join the pieced triangles made in Step 1, forming a pieced Butterfly square (Figure 4).

3. Repeat steps 1 and 2 as many times as you need to make enough pieces for your quilt-top.

4. Alternating Butterfly squares and solid squares (Square 3), make rows and then sew the rows together to make the quilt-top (see Figure 1).

4. Join the pieced triangles to make a Butterfly square.

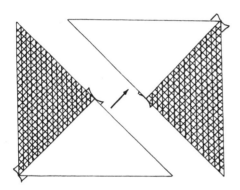

3. Make two pieced triangles.

Churn Dash

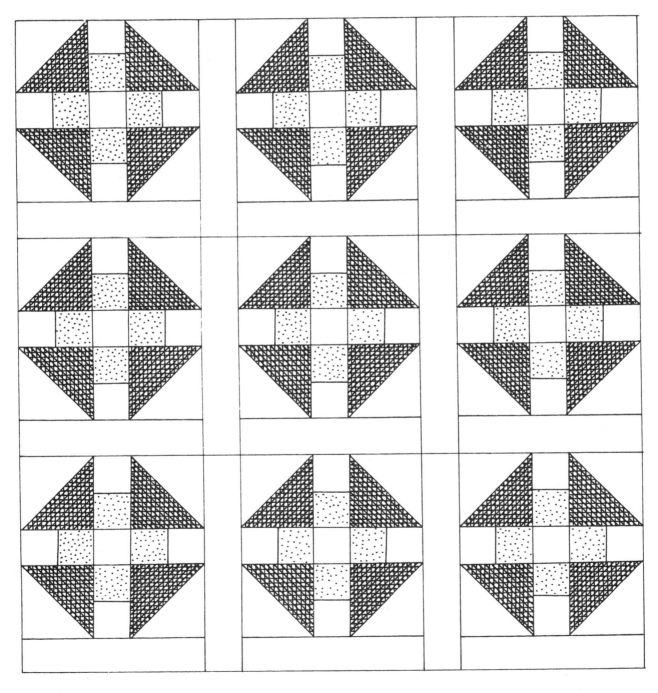

1. The Churn Dash quilt-top.

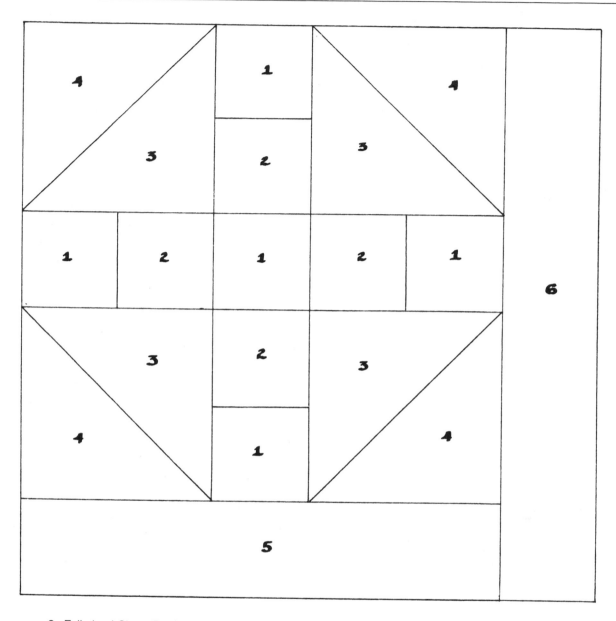

2. Full-sized Churn Dash Block. Seam allowances are not included. Size: 6″ × 6″ (15.2 cm × 15.2 cm).

Directions

Trace the template patterns onto template cardboard or plastic and cut out the templates. Do not add seam allowance to the template. As you trace around the templates on your fabric, add ¼″ (.6 cm) seam allowance around each piece. Cut out the pieces from the fabric. All piecing is done with right sides of material facing and with seam allowances of ¼″ (.6 cm). Press seam allowances open after each new piece is added. To piece the Churn Dash Block (Figure 2):

1. Join Triangle 3 to Triangle 4 by their long sides to form a pieced square (Figure 3).

2. Repeat Step 1 three more times to make the 4 pieced squares you will need for the Churn Dash Block.

3. Join Square 1 to Square 2 to make a pieced rectangle (Figure 4). Make 3 more rectangles the same way.

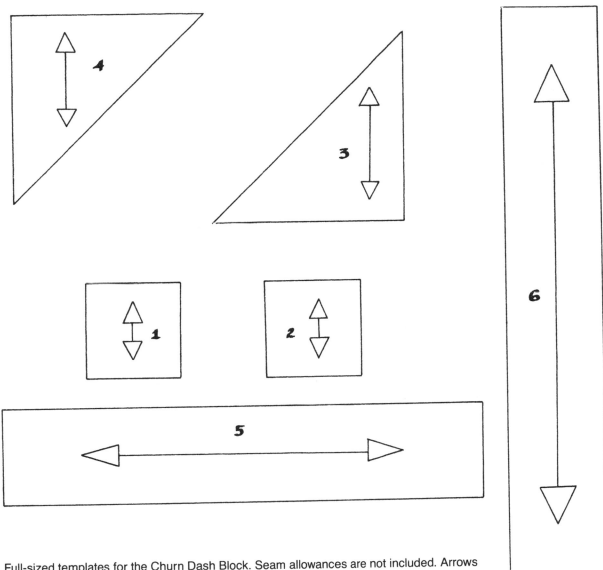

Full-sized templates for the Churn Dash Block. Seam allowances are not included. Arrows indicate straight grain of fabric.

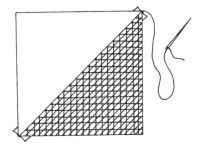

3. Join Triangle 3 to Triangle 4.

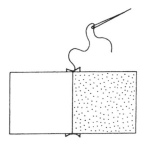

4. Join Square 1 to Square 2.

4. Take two of the pieced squares you made in Step 1 and one of the pieced rectangles you made in Step 3. Join them as shown in Figure 5. This completes one side unit of the Churn Dash square.

5. Repeat Step 4 to make another side unit.

6. Take a Square 1 and two pieced rectangles made in Step 3. Sew them together as shown in Figure 6.

7. Take the two side units you made in steps 4 and 5, and the strip of squares you made in Step 6. Join them as shown in Figure 7 to complete the Churn Dash square (Figure 8).

8. Attach a Rectangle 5 to the bottom of the Churn Dash square (Figure 9).

9. Attach a Rectangle 6 to the side of the unit you made in Step 8 to complete the Churn Dash Block (Figure 10).

10. Make as many blocks as you need for your quilt-top material and piece them as shown in Figure 1.

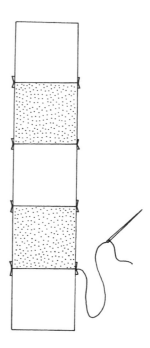

6. Join two pieced rectangles to Square 1 as shown to make a strip of five squares.

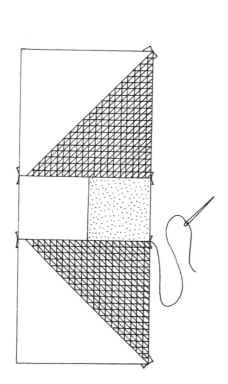

5. Join two pieced squares to a pieced rectangle to make a side unit of the block.

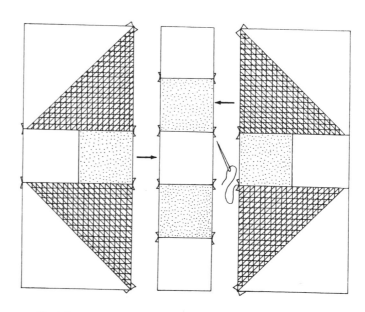

7. Join two pieced side units to a strip of five squares to create a Churn Dash square.

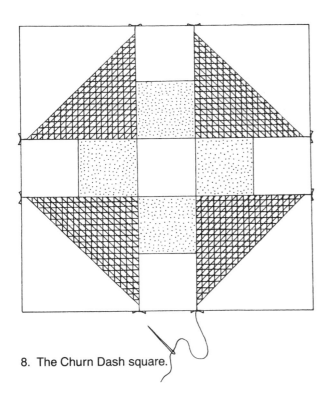

8. The Churn Dash square.

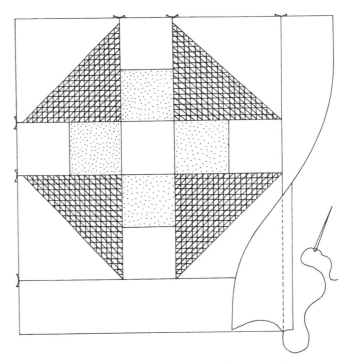

10. Attach Rectangle 6 to complete the Churn Dash block.

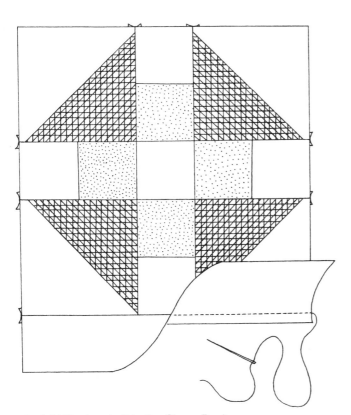

9. Add Rectangle 5 to the Churn Dash square.

Flyfoot

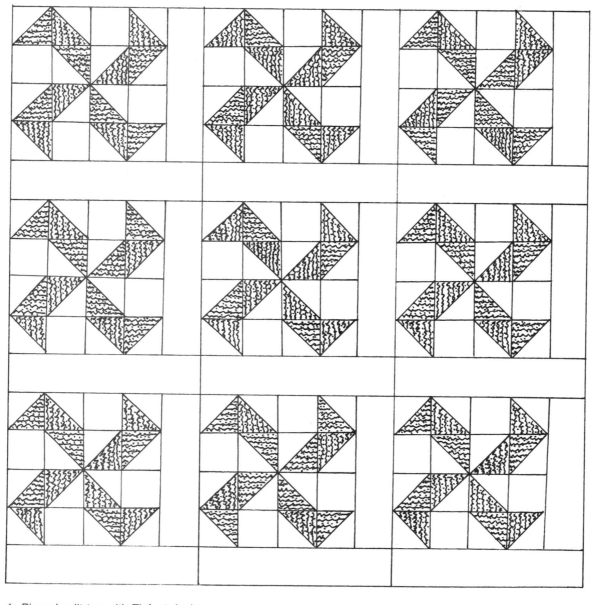

1. Pieced quilt-top with Flyfoot design.

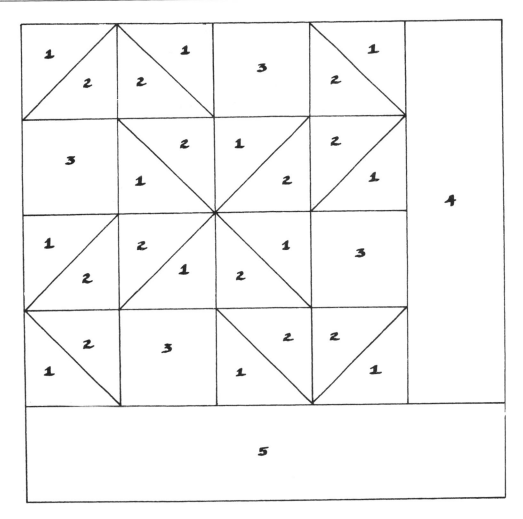

2. Full-sized piecing diagram for Flyfoot Block. Size: 5″ × 5″ (12.7 cm × 12.7 cm) without seam allowances.

Directions

Trace the template patterns onto template cardboard or plastic and cut out the templates. Do not add seam allowances to the templates. As you trace around the templates on your fabric, add ¼″ (.6 cm) seam allowance around each piece. Cut out the pieces from the fabric.

All piecing is done with right sides of material facing and with seam allowances of ¼″ (.6 cm). Press seam allowances open after each new piece is added. In our model, the solid squares (Square 3) and the Triangle 1 pieces are the same color. To make a Flyfoot Block (Figure 2):

1. Join Triangle 1 to Triangle 2 on their long sides to make a pieced square (Figure 3). Make 11 more pieced squares the same way.

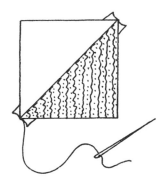

3. Join Triangle 1 to Triangle 2 on their long sides.

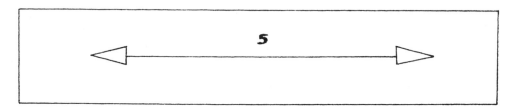

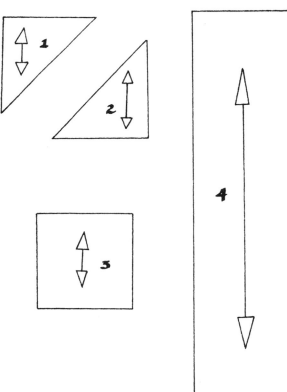

Full-sized templates for the Flyfoot Block. Seam allowances are not included. Arrows indicate straight grain of fabric.

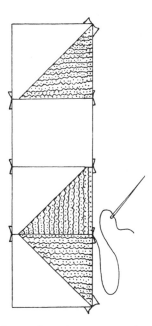

4. Join three pieced squares and one solid square (Square 3), as shown.

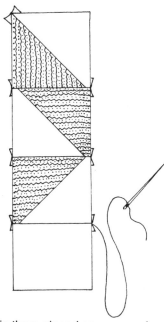

5. Join three pieced squares and one solid square, as shown.

2. Take 3 of the pieced squares you made in Step 1 and one Square 3 (solid-colored square). Join them as shown in Figure 4 to make the leftmost columm of the block.

3. Repeat Step 2 to make the rightmost (4th) column of the block. It will be turned upside down when pieced.

4. Take 3 more of the pieced squares you made in Step 1, plus one Square 3. Join them as shown in Figure 5 to make column 2 of the Flyfoot Block.

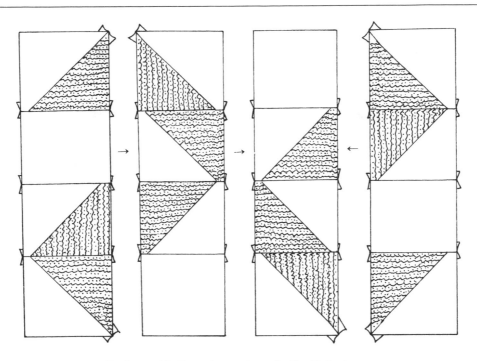

6. Assemble the columns to make the Flyfoot square.

5. Repeat Step 4 to make column 3 of the Flyfoot square. It will be turned upside down when it is pieced.

6. Position the columns you made in steps 2–5 as shown in Figure 6, and join them (Figure 7).

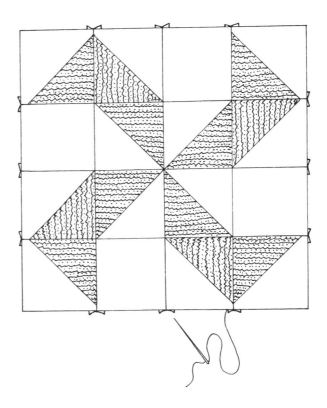

7. The assembled Flyfoot square.

7. Attach Rectangle 4 to the right of the Flyfoot square completed in Step 6 (Figure 8).

8. Attach Rectangle 5 to the unit you created in Step 7 (see Figure 9). This completes the Flyfoot Block.

9. Make as many blocks as you need to piece the material for your quilt-top. Assemble them as shown in Figure 1.

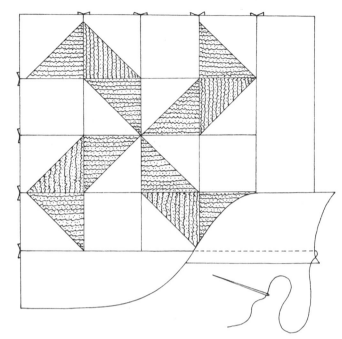

9. Add Rectangle 5 to complete the Flyfoot Block.

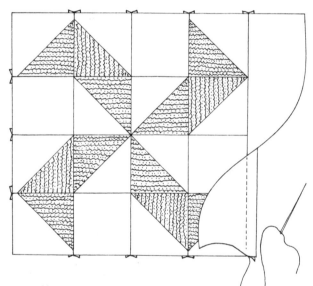

8. Add Rectangle 4 to the Flyfoot square at right.

Kansas Dugout

Directions

Trace the template patterns onto template cardboard or plastic and cut out the templates. Do not add seam allowances to the templates. As you trace around the templates on your fabric, add ¼″ (.6 cm) seam allowance around each piece. Cut out the pieces from the fabric.

All piecing is done with right sides of material facing and with seam allowances of ¼″ (.6 cm). Press seam allowances open after each new piece is added.

In our model, Square 2 and Triangle 1 are made of the same color and pattern of fabric. To piece the Kansas Dugout Block (Figure 2):

1. Join Triangle 4 and Triangle 1 on their long sides to make a pieced square (Figure 3). Make 3 more pieced squares in the same way.

2. Take two pieced squares made in Step 1 and one Square 2. Join them as shown in Figure 4, left. Make another unit the same way for the right column of the Kansas Dugout (Figure 4, right).

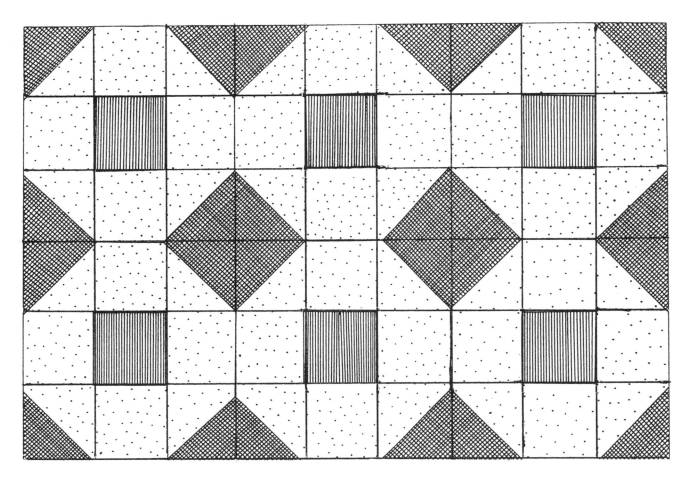

1. Pieced quilt-top with Kansas Dugout design.

151

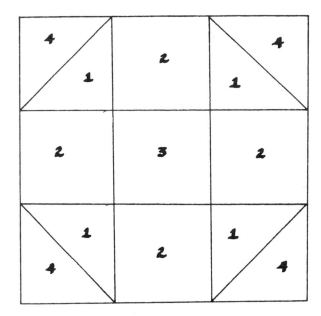

2. Full-sized pattern of the Kansas Dugout Block. Size: 3″ × 3″ (7.6 cm × 7.6 cm). Seam allowances are not included.

3. Take two of Square 2 and one of Square 3. Join them as shown in Figure 4, center.

4. Join the three columns made in steps 2 and 3 to form a Kansas Dugout Block (Figure 5).

5. Make as many Kansas Dugout blocks as you need for the quilt-top. Join them as shown in Figure 1.

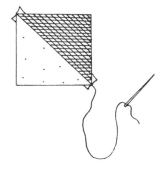

3. Join Triangle 1 to Triangle 4 on their long sides.

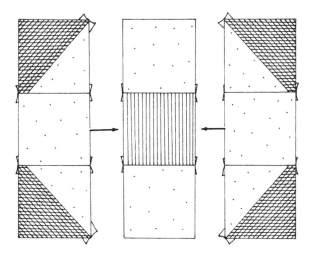

4. The three pieced columns that make up the Kansas Dugout Block.

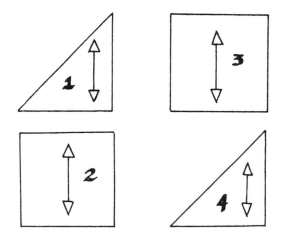

Full-sized templates for the Kansas Dugout Block. Templates do not include seam allowances. Arrows indicate straight grain of fabric.

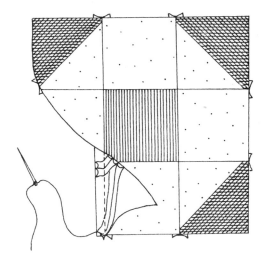

5. Join the columns to form the block.

Clay's Choice

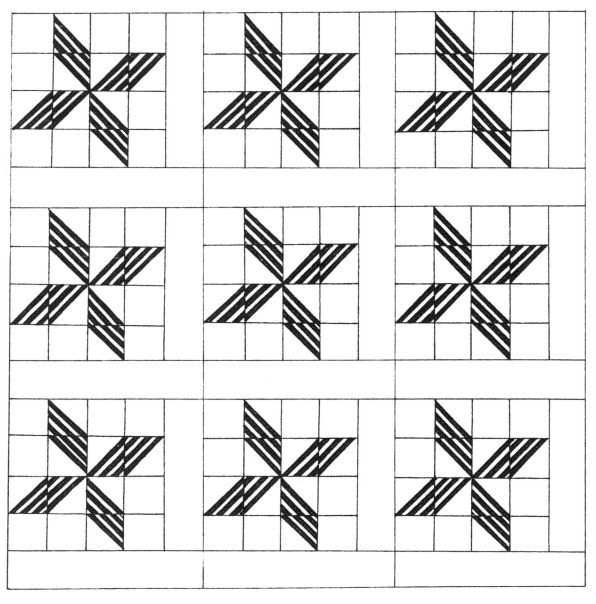

1. The Clay's Choice quilt-top.

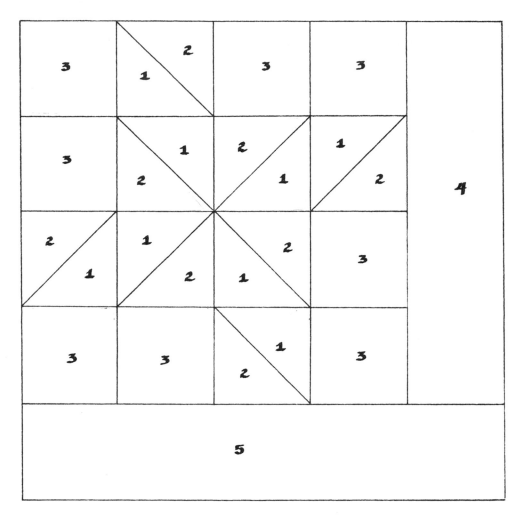

2. Full-sized Clay's Choice Block. Seam allowances are not included. Size: 5″ × 5″ (12.7 cm × 12.7 cm).

Directions

Trace the template patterns onto template cardboard or plastic and cut out the templates. Do not add seam allowances to the templates. As you trace around the templates on your fabric, add ¼″ (.6 cm) seam allowance around each piece. Cut out the pieces from the fabric.

All piecing is done with right sides of material facing and with seam allowances of ¼″ (.6 cm). Press seam allowances open after each new piece is added. In our model, Square 3 and Triangle 2 are made of the same color fabric. To piece the Clay's Choice Block (Figure 2):

1. Sew Triangle 1 to Triangle 2 on their long sides to make a pieced square (Figure 3).

2. Repeat Step 1 seven more times for a total of 8 pieced squares.

3. Take eight of Square 3 and the eight pieced squares you made. Form them into columns as described below:
   A. To make the leftmost column (Column 1) of the block, join three of Square 3 (the solid square) and one pieced square as shown in Figure 4.

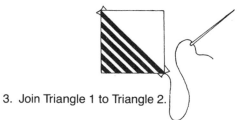

3. Join Triangle 1 to Triangle 2.

B. For column 2, join three pieced squares and one Square 3 as shown in Figure 5.

C. Repeat Step B to form column 3. It will be turned upside down when it is pieced (Figure 6).

D. Repeat Step A to form column 4. It will be turned upside down when pieced.

4. Place the columns made in Step 3 as shown in Figure 6, and sew them together.

5. Attach Rectangle 4 as shown in Figure 7.

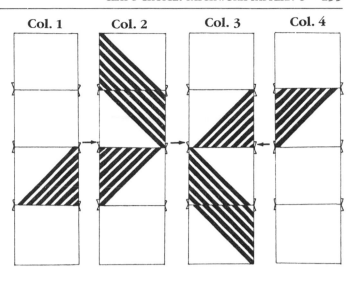

Col. 1   Col. 2   Col. 3   Col. 4

6. Lay out the 4 columns as shown and sew them together.

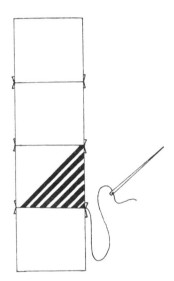

4. Piece the leftmost column of the block as shown.

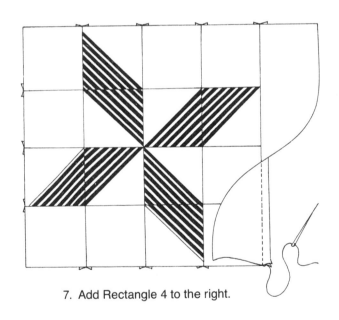

7. Add Rectangle 4 to the right.

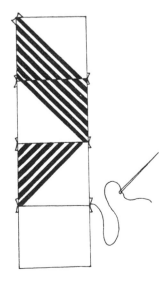

5. Piece column 2 as shown.

6. Attach Rectangle 5 as shown in Figure 8. This completes the Clay's Choice Block.

7. Make as many blocks as you need for your quilt-top and join them as shown in Figure 1.

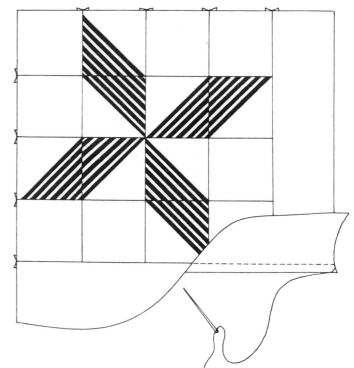

8. Add Rectangle 5 to the bottom to complete the block.

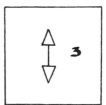

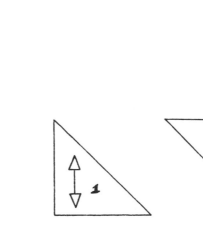

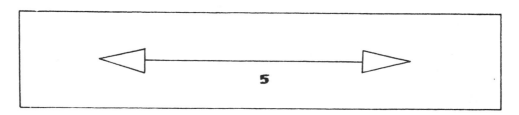

Full-sized templates for Clay's Choice Block. Seam allowances are not included. Arrows indicate straight grain of fabric.

Shoo-Fly

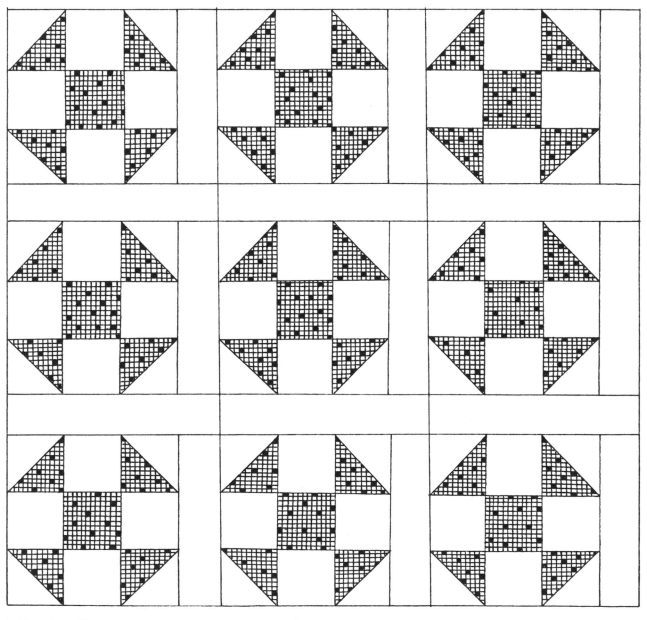

1. The Shoo-Fly quilt-top.

Directions

Trace the template patterns onto template cardboard or plastic and cut out the templates. Do not add seam allowances to the templates. As you trace around the templates on your fabric, add ¼″ (.6 cm) seam allowance around each piece. Cut out the pieces from the fabric.

All piecing is done with right sides of material facing and with seam allowances of ¼″ (.6 cm). Press seam allowances open after each new piece is added. To piece the Shoo-Fly Block (Figure 2):

1. Join Triangle 1 to Triangle 2 on their long sides (Figure 3) to make a pieced square. Make three more pieced squares the same way.

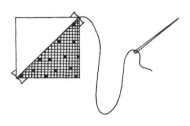

3. Join Triangle 1 to Triangle 2 on their long sides.

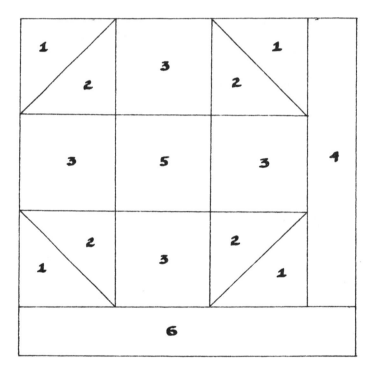

2. Full-sized Shoo-Fly Block. Seam allowances are not included. Size: 3½″ × 3½″ (8.9 cm × 8.9 cm).

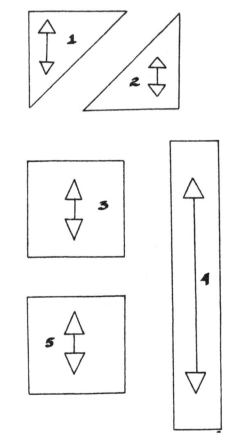

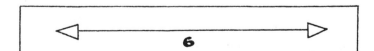

Full-sized templates for the Shoo-Fly Block. Seam allowances are not included. Arrows indicate straight grain of fabric.

2. Take four of Square 3 and one of Square 5 plus the pieced squares you made in Step 1. Sew them into 3 columns as shown in Figure 4:

A. Left column: pieced square, Square 3, pieced square.

B. Middle column: Square 3, Square 5, Square 3.

C. Right column: pieced square, Square 3, pieced square.

3. Join the columns to make a Shoo-Fly Square (Figure 5).

4. Add Rectangle 4 at the right (Figure 6).

5. Add Rectangle 6 at the bottom (Figure 7) to complete the Shoo-Fly Block.

6. Make as many Shoo-Fly Blocks as you need for your quilt-top material; piece them as shown in Figure 1.

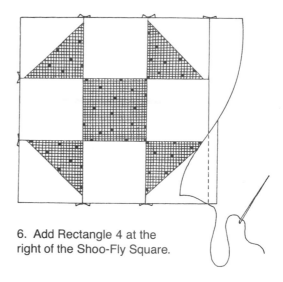

6. Add Rectangle 4 at the right of the Shoo-Fly Square.

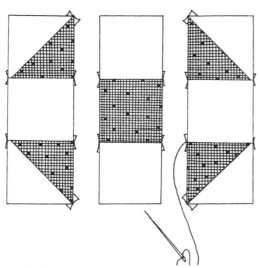

4. Join the squares into three columns.

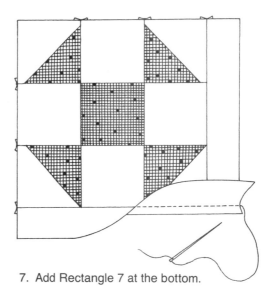

7. Add Rectangle 7 at the bottom.

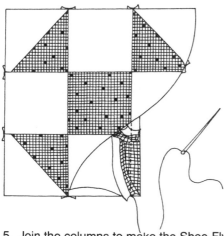

5. Join the columns to make the Shoo-Fly square.

Ohio Star

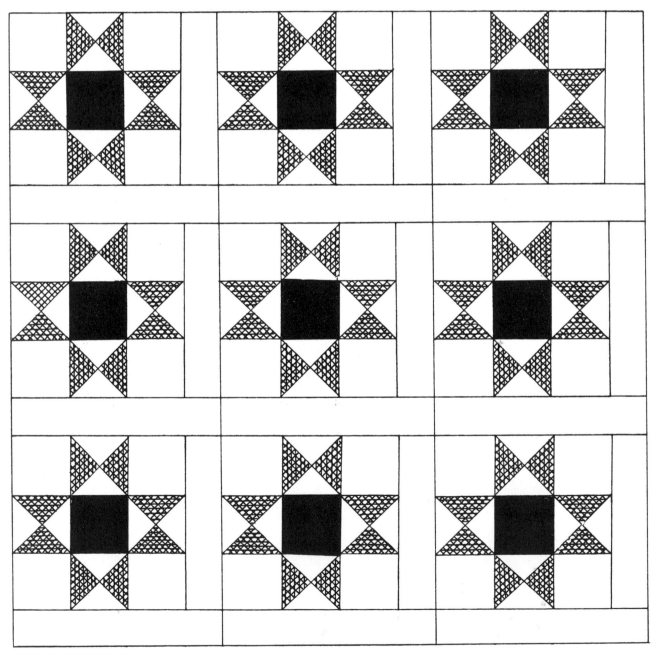

1. The Ohio Star quilt-top.

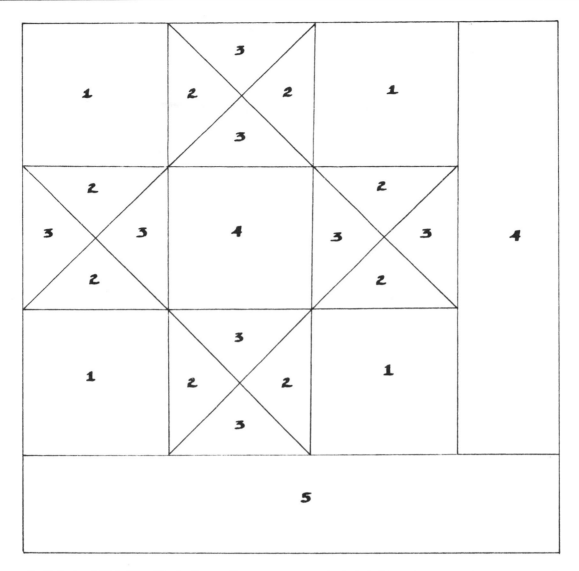

2. Full-sized Ohio Star Block. Seam allowances are not included. Size: 5½" × 5½" (14 cm × 14 cm).

Directions

Trace the template patterns onto template cardboard or plastic and cut out the templates. Do not add seam allowances to the templates. As you trace around the templates on your fabric, add ¼" (.6 cm) seam allowance around each piece. Cut out the pieces from the fabric.

All piecing is done with right sides of material facing and with seam allowances ,of ¼" (.6 cm). Press seam allowances open after each new piece is added. To piece the Ohio Star Block (Figure 2):

1. Join Triangle 2 to Triangle 3 on their short sides to make a pieced triangle (Figure 3). Make 7 more pieced triangles the same way.

3. Join Triangle 2 to Triangle 3 on their short sides to make a pieced triangle.

2. Join two of the pieced triangles you made in Step 1 to make a pieced square (Figure 4).

3. Take two of Square 1 and attach them to the top and bottom of the pieced square you made in Step 2 (Figure 5). This will make the left column of the Ohio Star square.

4. Take two pieced squares and join one above and one below Square 4 (Figure 6) to make the middle column of the Ohio Star square.

5. Repeat Step 3 to make the right column of the Ohio Star square (Figure 7, right).

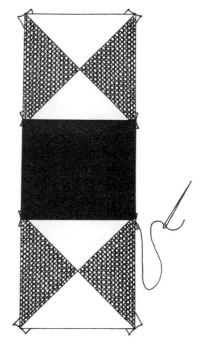

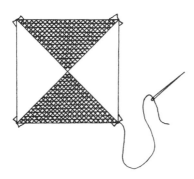

4. Join two pieced triangles to make a pieced square.

6. Attach a pieced square above and below Square 4 to make the middle column of the Ohio Star square.

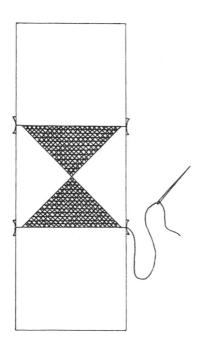

5. Attach a Square 1 above and below a pieced square to make the left column of the Star square. Repeat for the right column.

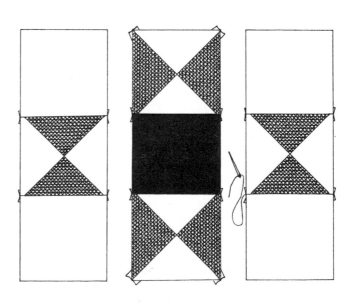

7. Three columns for the Ohio Star square.

6. Piece the three columns, shown in Figure 7, to make the Ohio Star square (Figure 8).

7. Add Rectangle 4 to the right of the Ohio Star square (Figure 9).

8. Add Rectangle 5 to the bottom (Figure 10) of the unit made in Step 7 to complete the Ohio Star Block.

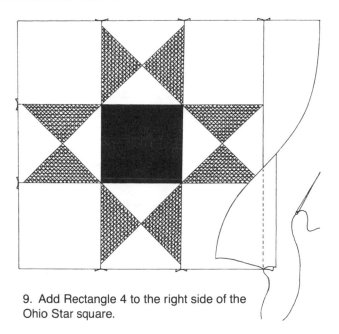

9. Add Rectangle 4 to the right side of the Ohio Star square.

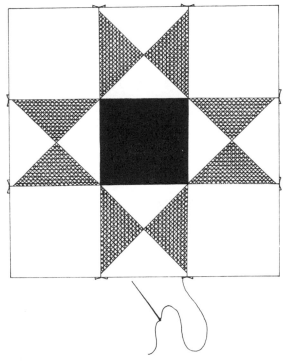

8. The three columns joined in an Ohio Star square.

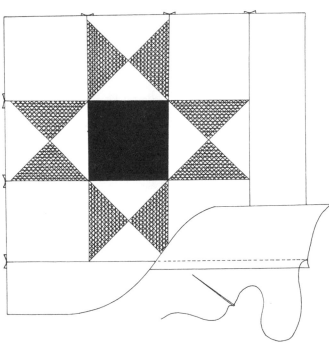

10. Add Rectangle 5 below the unit you pieced in Step 7.

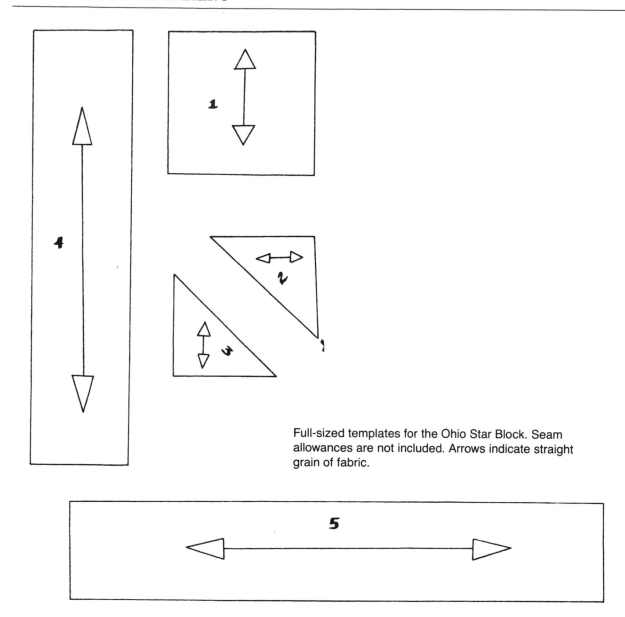

Full-sized templates for the Ohio Star Block. Seam allowances are not included. Arrows indicate straight grain of fabric.

Pinwheel

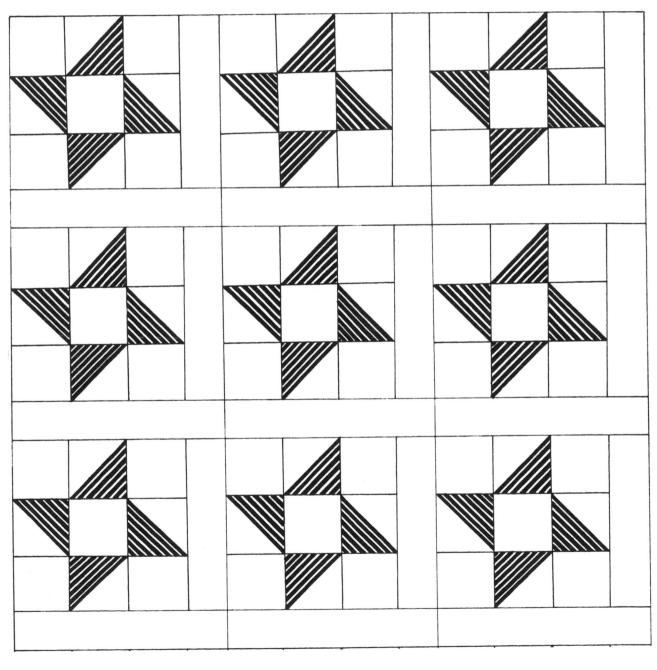

1. The Pinwheel quilt-top.

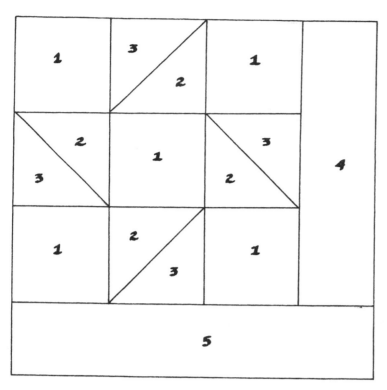

2. The full-sized Pinwheel Block. Seam allowances are not included. Size: 3¾" × 3¾" (9.5 cm × 9.5 cm).

Directions

Trace the template patterns onto template cardboard or plastic and cut out the templates. Do not add seam allowances to the templates. As you trace around the templates on your fabric, add ¼" (.6 cm) seam allowance around each piece. Cut out the pieces from the fabric.

All piecing is done with right sides of material facing and with seam allowances of ¼" (.6 cm). Press seam allowances open after each new piece is added. To piece the Pinwheel Block (Figure 2):

1. Join Triangle 2 to Triangle 3 on their long sides to make a pieced square (Figure 3). Make three more pieced squares the same way.

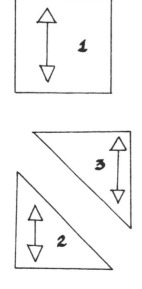

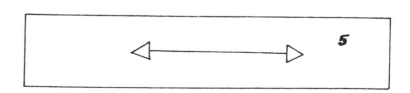

Full-sized templates for the Pinwheel Block. Seam allowances are not included. Arrows indicate straight grain of fabric.

2. Take the four pieced squares and five of Square 1. Join them in three columns as follows (see Figure 4 for positioning):

   A. Left column: Square 1, pieced square, Square 1.

   B. Middle column: pieced square, Square 1, pieced square.

   C. Right column: Square 1, pieced square, Square 1.

3. Join the columns to make the Pinwheel square (Figure 5).

4. Attach Rectangle 4 to the right of the Pinwheel square (Figure 6).

5. Attach Rectangle 5 to the bottom of the unit you pieced in Step 4 to complete the Pinwheel Block (Figure 7).

6. Make as many Pinwheel Blocks as you need for your quilt-top, and join them as shown in Figure 1.

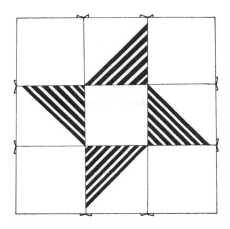

5. Join the columns to make the Pinwheel square.

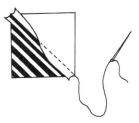

3. Join Triangle 2 to Triangle 3 on their long sides to make a pieced square.

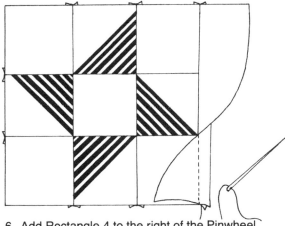

6. Add Rectangle 4 to the right of the Pinwheel square.

4. Piece the three columns that make the Pinwheel square.

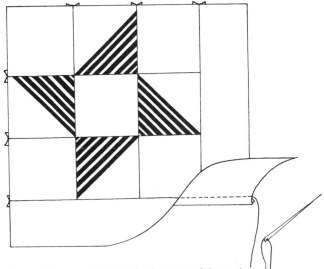

7. Add Rectangle 5 to the bottom of the unit to complete the Pinwheel Block.

Square in Diamond in Square

1. The Square in Diamond in Square quilt-top.

Directions

Trace the template patterns onto template cardboard or plastic and cut out the templates. Do not add seam allowances to the templates. As you trace around the templates on your fabric, add ¼" (.6 cm) seam allowance around each piece. Cut out the pieces from the fabric.

All piecing is done with right sides of material facing and with seam allowances of ¼" (.6 cm). Press seam allowances open after each new piece is added. To piece the Square in Diamond in Square Block (Figure 2):

1. Take Square 1 and four of Triangle 2. Join the triangles to Square 1 on their long sides (Figure 3).

2. Take 4 of Triangle 3 and join them on their long sides to the unit you made in Step 1 (Figure 4). This completes the Square in Diamond in Square Block.

3. Make as many Square in Diamond in Square blocks as you need for your quilt-top material (see Figure 1).

4. Alternate them with solid blocks (Figure 5) and piece the rows as shown in Figure 1. Join the rows to make the quilt-top material.

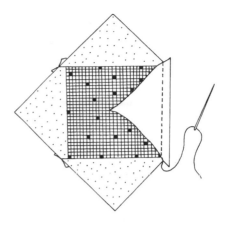

3. Join four of Triangle 2 to Square 1 on their long sides to make the square in diamond.

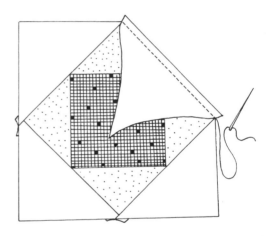

4. Attach four of Triangle 3 on their long sides to the square in diamond.

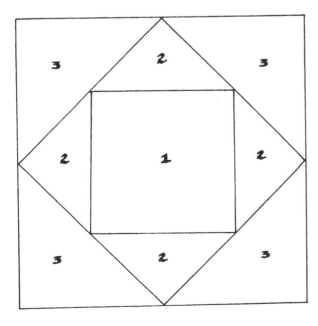

2. Full-sized Square in Diamond in Square Block. Seam allowances are not included. Size: 3" × 3" (7.6 cm × 7.6 cm).

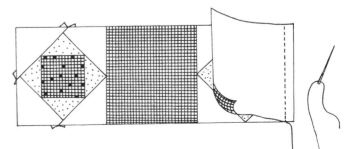

5. Alternate the Square in Diamond in Square blocks with solid squares to make the pattern shown in Figure 1.

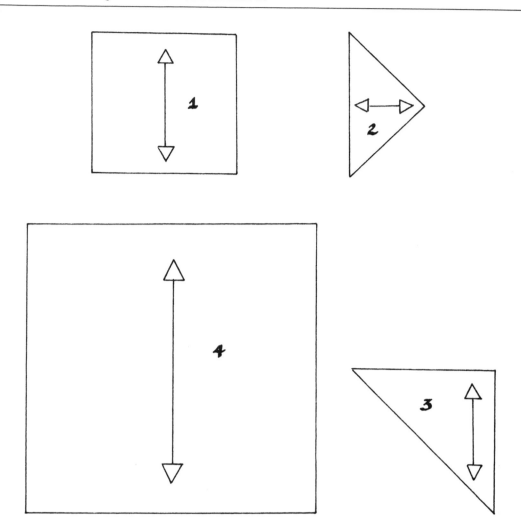

1–3. Full-sized templates for the Square in Diamond in Square Block. 4 is the solid square. Seam allowances are not included. Arrows indicate straight grain of fabric.

Flying Geese

1. The Flying Geese quilt-top.

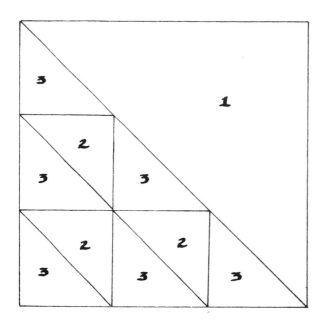

2. The full-sized Flying Geese Block. Seam allowances are not included. Size: 3″ × 3″ (7.6 cm × 7.6 cm).

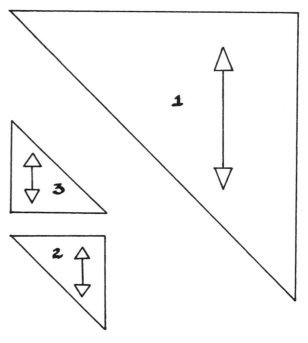

Full-sized templates for the Flying Geese Block. Seam allowances are not included. Arrows indicate straight grain of fabric.

Directions

Trace the template patterns onto template cardboard or plastic and cut out the templates. Do not add seam allowances to the templates. As you trace around the templates on your fabric, add ¼″ (.6 cm) seam allowance around each piece. Cut out the pieces from the fabric.

All piecing is done with right sides of material facing and with seam allowances of ¼″ (.6 cm). Press seam allowances open after each new piece is added. To piece the Flying Geese Block (Figure 2), first we will create the large pieced triangle at the lower left of the block:

1. Join Triangle 3 to Triangle 2 on their long sides (Figure 3) to make a pieced square. Make two more pieced squares the same way.

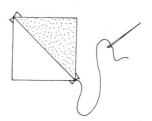

3. Join Triangle 3 to Triangle 2 on their long sides.

2. Join two pieced squares from Step 1 and a Triangle 3 to make the leftmost column of the large pieced triangle (see Figure 4).

3. Join a Triangle 3 to a pieced square from Step 1, as shown in Figure 5, to make the middle column of the large pieced triangle (Figure 5).

4. Join the leftmost and middle columns of the large pieced triangle as shown in Figure 6.

5. Add a Triangle 3 as shown in Figure 7 to complete the large pieced triangle.

6. Join Triangle 1 to the large pieced triangle to complete the Flying Geese Block (Figure 8).

7. Make as many blocks as you need and join them as shown in Figure 1 to complete the quilt-top material.

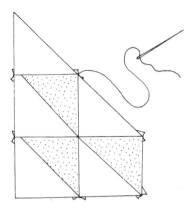

6. Join the leftmost and middle columns of the large pieced triangle.

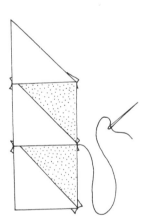

4. Join two pieced squares and a Triangle 3 to make the leftmost column of the large pieced triangle.

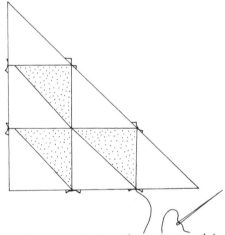

7. Add a Triangle 3 as shown to complete the large pieced triangle.

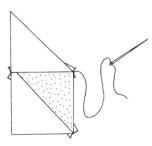

5. Join a Triangle 3 to a pieced square to make the middle column of the large pieced triangle.

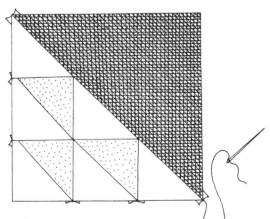

8. Join Triangle 1 and a large pieced triangle on their long sides to complete the block.

Maple Leaf

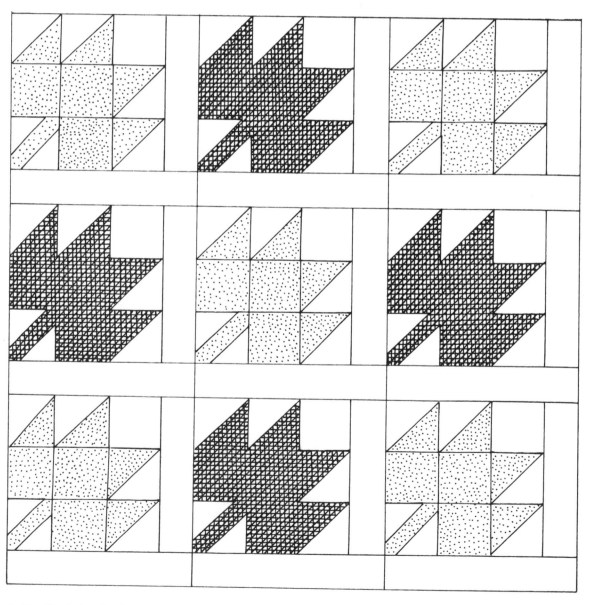

1. The Maple Leaf quilt-top.

The pattern in Figure 1 is made by having a common color for Triangle 1 and Square 3 for all blocks and changing the color of Triangle 2, Square 4, and Strip 5 on alternate blocks of the quilt-top.

Directions

Trace the template patterns onto template cardboard or plastic and cut out the templates. Do not add seam allowances to the templates. As you trace around the templates on your fabric, add ¼" (.6 cm) seam allowance around each piece. Cut out the pieces from the fabric.

All piecing is done with right sides of material facing and with seam allowances of ¼" (.6 cm). Press seam allowances open after each new piece is added. To piece the Maple Leaf Block (Figure 2):

1. Join Triangle 1 to Triangle 2 on their long sides to form a pieced square (Figure 3). Make three more pieced squares the same way.

2. Take Square 3 and baste and appliqué Rectangle 5 to it as shown in Figure 4 to make the stem square of the maple leaf. Trim off the excess fabric after appliquéing is done.

3. Take three of Square 4 and 1 of Square 3, plus

the pieced squares you made in Step 1. Join them in three columns as shown in Figure 5:

A. Left column: pieced square, Square 4, stem square.

B. Middle column: pieced square, Square 4, Square 4.

C. Right column: Square 3, pieced square, pieced square.

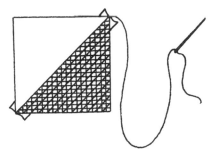

3. Join Triangle 1 to Triangle 2 on their long sides.

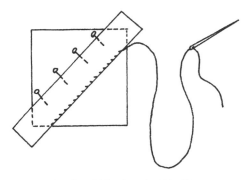

4. Appliqué Rectangle 5 to Square 3. Trim off excess fabric that extends over the square.

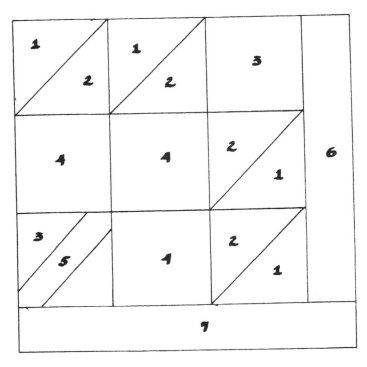

2. Full-sized Maple Leaf Block. Seam allowances are not included. Size: 3½" × 3½" (8.9 cm × 8.9 cm). Strip 5 is appliquéd over Square 3.

5. Join the squares in columns as shown.

4. Join the columns to form a Maple Leaf square and add Rectangle 6 at the right (Figure 6).

5. Attach Rectangle 7 to the bottom of the unit you made in Step 4 to complete the Maple Leaf Block (Figure 7).

6. Make as many blocks as you need for your quilt-top material and piece them as shown in Figure 1.

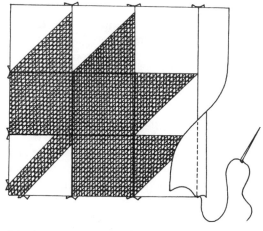

6. Join the columns to make the Maple Leaf square. Attach Rectangle 6 at the right.

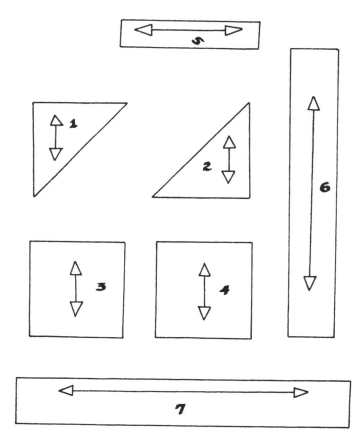

Full-sized templates for the Maple Leaf Block. Seam allowances are not included. Arrows indicate straight grain of fabric.

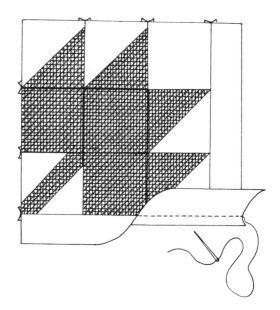

7. Add Rectangle 7 at the bottom to complete the Maple Leaf Block.

T-Block

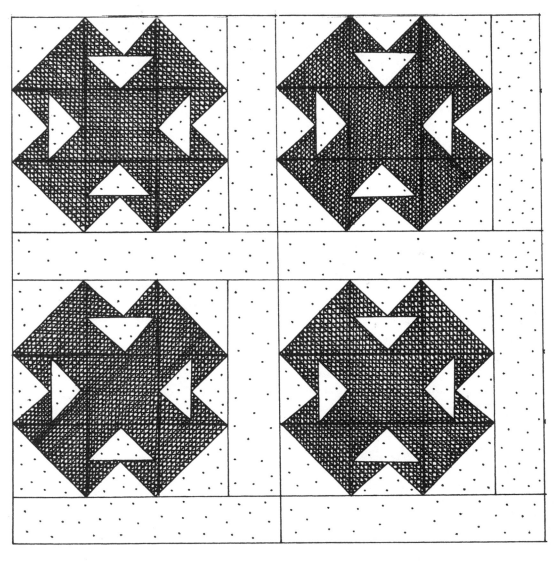

1. The T-Block quilt-top.

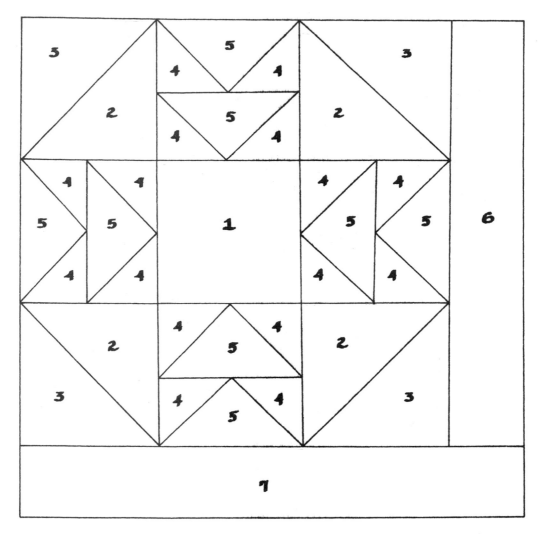

2. The full-sized T-Block. Seam allowances **are not included. Size:** 5¼″ × 5¼″ (13.3 cm × 13.3 cm).

Directions

Trace the template patterns onto template cardboard or plastic and cut out the templates. Do not add seam allowances to the templates. As you trace around the templates on your fabric, add ¼″ (.6 cm) seam allowance around each piece. Cut out the pieces from the fabric.

All piecing is done with right sides of material facing and with seam allowances of ¼″ (.6 cm). Iron seam allowances open after each new piece is added. To piece the T-Block (Figure 2):

1. Join Triangle 2 to Triangle 3 on their long sides to make a large pieced square. Make 3 more pieced squares in the same way (Figure 3). Set them aside.

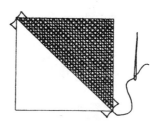

3. Join Triangle 2 to Triangle 3 on their long sides.

2. Join a Triangle 4 on its long side to a short side of Triangle 5 (Figure 4). Join another Triangle 4 on the other short side of Triangle 5 (Figure 5) to complete the pieced rectangle.

3. Make 7 more pieced rectangles just like the one you made in Step 2.

4. Join two pieced rectangles together to make Unit A, shown in Figure 6. Make 3 more of Unit A in the same way.

5. To make the left column of the T-square, take two pieced squares made in Step 1, and a Unit A, made in Step 4. Join them as shown in Figure 7.

6. To make the middle column of the T-square, take two of Unit A and one Square 1. Join one Unit A to the top of Square 1 and one to the bottom, as shown in Figure 8.

7. To make the right column of the T-square, repeat Step 5. The piece will be turned upside-down when pieced (see Figure 9).

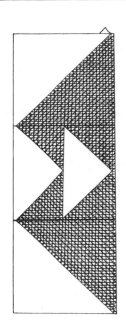
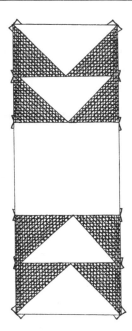

7. Attach a pieced square above and below Unit A.

8. Attach one Unit A to the top and one to the bottom of Square 1.

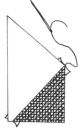

4. Join Triangle 4 on its long side to a short side of Triangle 5.

5. A pieced rectangle unit, made from two of Triangle 4 and one of Triangle 5.

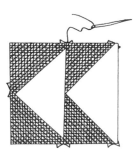

6. Join two pieced rectangle units to form Unit A.

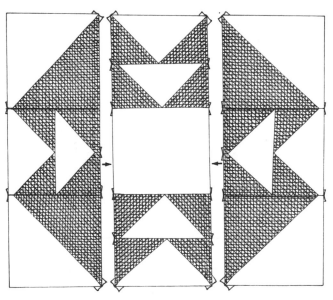

9. The three columns of the T-square.

8. Position the three columns of the T-square as shown in Figure 9, and sew them together.

9. Attach Rectangle 6 at the right of the T-square (Figure 10).

10. Attach Rectangle 7 at the bottom of the unit to complete the T-Block (Figure 11).

11. Make as many T-Blocks as you need for the quilt-top material, and piece them together as shown in Figure 1.

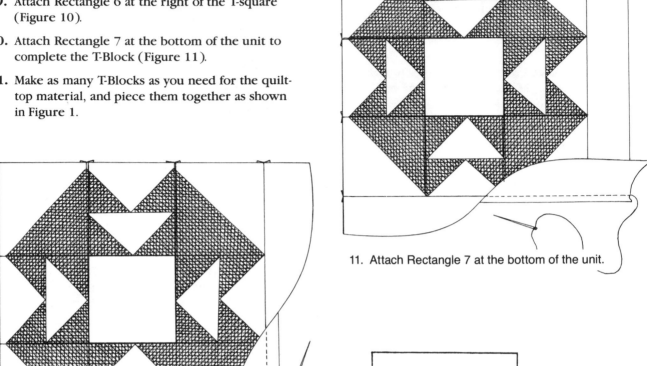

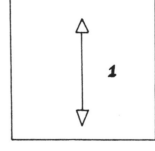

11. Attach Rectangle 7 at the bottom of the unit.

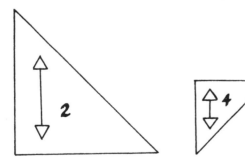

10. Attach Rectangle 6 at the right of the T-square.

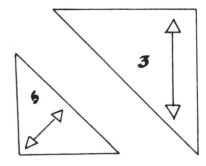

Full-sized T-Block templates. Seam allowances are not included. Arrows indicate the straight grain of the fabric.

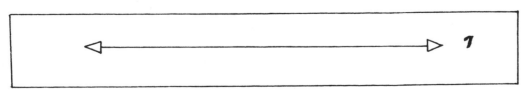

Navajo Star

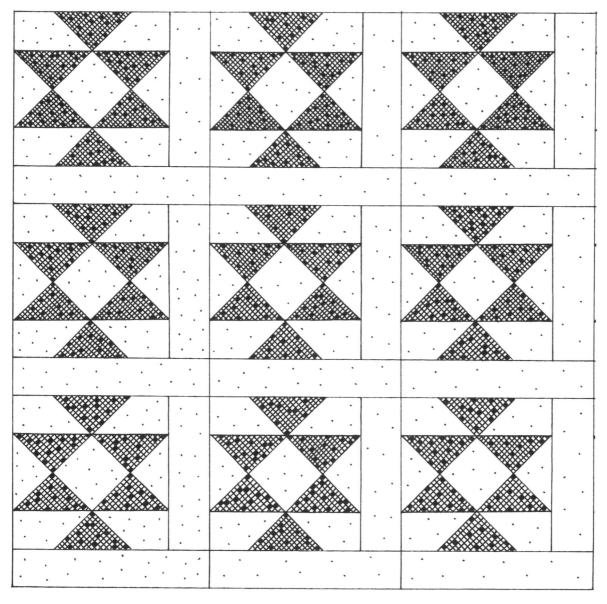

1. The Navajo Star quilt-top.

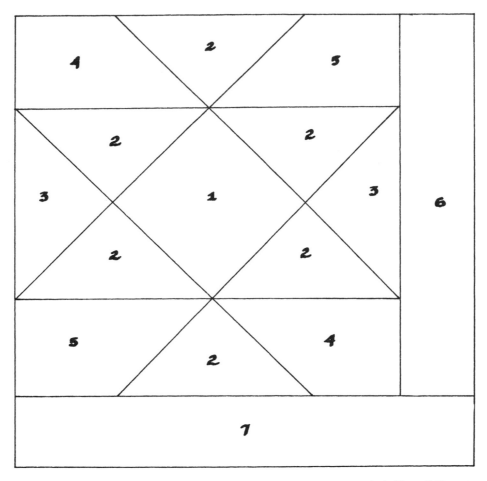

2. Full-sized Navajo Star Block. Seam allowances are not included. Size: 4¾″ × 4¾″ (10.8 cm × 10.8 cm).

Directions

Trace the template patterns onto template cardboard or plastic and cut out the templates. Do not add seam allowances to the templates. As you trace around the templates on your fabric, add ¼″ (.6 cm) seam allowance around each piece. Cut out the pieces from the fabric.

All piecing is done with right sides of material facing and with seam allowances of ¼″ (.6 cm). Iron seam allowances open after each new piece is added. To piece the Navajo Star (Figure 2), we will work in three horizontal strips:

1. *For Strip 1:* Attach Piece 4 to the left side of Triangle 2 and Piece 5 to the right side to form strip 1 (Figure 3).

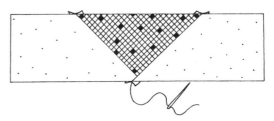

3. Join Piece 4 on the left side of Triangle 2 and Piece 5 on the right to make the first strip. Repeat for the third strip.

2. *For Strip 2:*

   A. Sew a Triangle 2 to a Triangle 3 on their short sides. Make another unit the same way (Figure 4, left and right).

   B. Sew a Triangle 2 on its short side to one side of Square 1 as shown in Figure 4, middle. Sew another Triangle 2 to the square's opposite side.

   C. Join the three parts of Strip 2 (see Figure 4) to complete Strip 2 (Figure 5).

3. *For Strip 3:* Repeat Step 1. The strip will be turned upside-down when joined.

4. Join the three strips to form the Navajo square (Figure 6).

5. Attach Rectangle 6 at the right of the Navajo square (Figure 7).

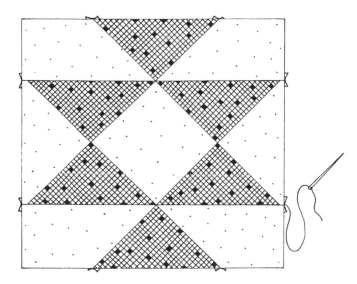

6. The Navajo Star design with the three strips sewn together.

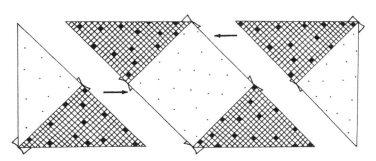

4. Join the three parts of Strip 2.

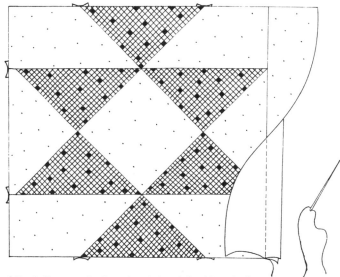

7. Attach Rectangle 6 at the right of the Navajo Star design.

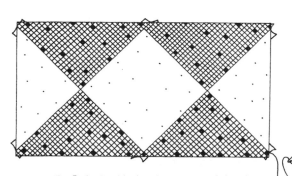

5. Strip 2 with the three parts joined.

6. Attach Rectangle 7 at the bottom of the unit pieced in Step 5 (Figure 8).

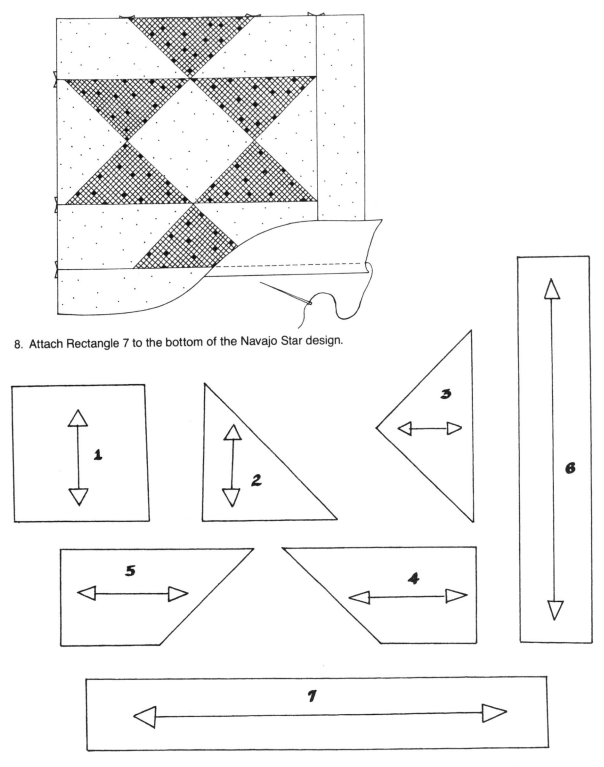

8. Attach Rectangle 7 to the bottom of the Navajo Star design.

Full-sized templates of the Navajo Star block. Seam allowances are not included. Arrows indicate straight grain of fabric.

Heart Leaves

1. The Heart Leaves quilt-top.

Directions

Trace the template patterns onto template cardboard or plastic and cut out the templates. Do not add seam allowances to the templates. As you trace around the templates on your fabric, add ¼″ (.6 cm) seam allowance around each piece. Cut out the pieces from the fabric.

All piecing is done with right sides of material facing and with seam allowances of ¼″ (.6 cm), except for the heart and stem shapes, which are appliquéd over the pieced triangles. Iron seam allowances open on triangles; iron appliqués flat after each new piece is added. To piece the Heart Leaves Block (Figure 2):

1. Attach Triangle 4 to Triangle 3 on their long sides (Figure 3) to make a pieced square. Set it aside.

2. Baste under the seam allowances of Rectangle 2 on its long sides (Figure 4). Set it aside.

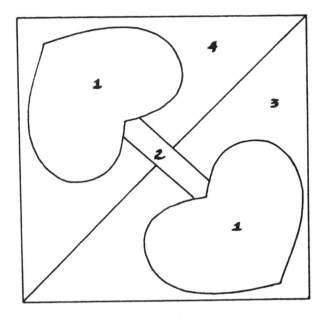

2. Full-sized Heart Leaves Block. Seam allowances are not included. 1 and 2 are appliquéd in place. Size: 3″ × 3″ (7.6 cm × 7.6 cm).

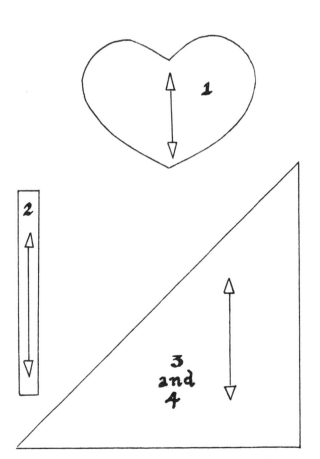

Full-sized templates for the Heart Leaves Block. Seam allowances are not included. Arrows indicate straight grain of fabric.

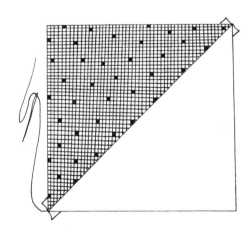

3. Seam Triangle 4 to Triangle 3 on their long sides.

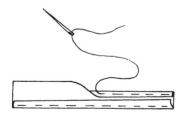

4. Baste the seam allowances under on the long sides of Rectangle 2.

3. Notch and baste the seam allowances under for two hearts (Piece 1); see Figure 5. Set them aside.

4. Pin Rectangle 2 (from Step 2) in place on the pieced square made in Step 1, as shown in Figure 6. Appliqué the rectangle in place.

5. Pin and appliqué the hearts prepared in Step 3 in place on the pieced square (Figure 7). They should cover the raw edges of the rectangle. This completes the Heart Leaves Block.

6. Make as many Heart Leaves Blocks as you need to complete your quilt-top material.

7. Join the pieced blocks in columns as shown in Figure 8; then join the columns to make the quilt-top.

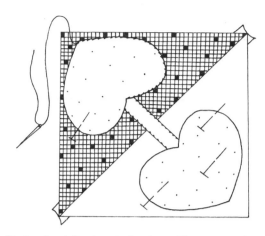

7. Appliqué the hearts in place. They cover the raw ends of Rectangle 2.

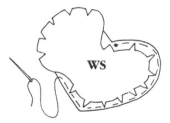

5. Notch and baste the seam allowance under on two hearts (Piece 1).

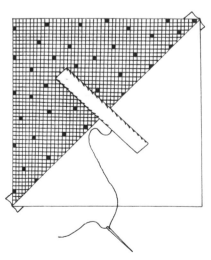

6. Appliqué Rectangle 2 in place.

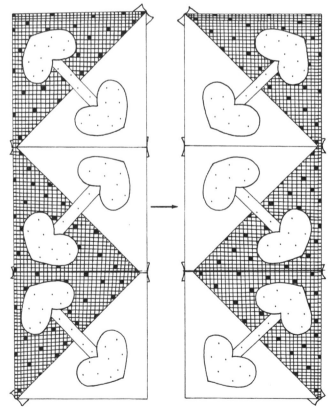

8. Join the blocks in columns; join the columns to make the quilt-top.

Waterwheel

1. The Waterwheel quilt-top.

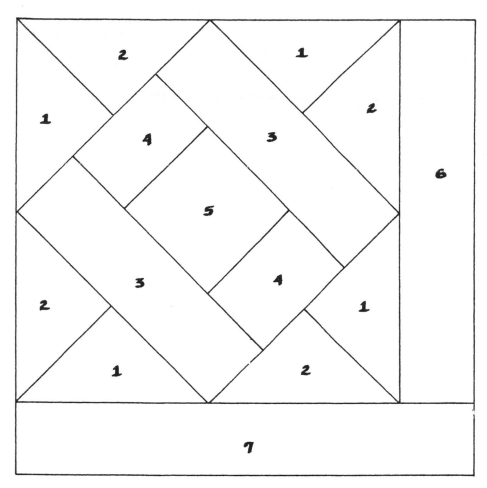

2. Full-sized Waterwheel Block. Seam allowances are not included. Size: 4¾" × 4¾" (12.1 cm × 12.1 cm).

Directions

Trace the template patterns onto template cardboard or plastic and cut out the templates. Do not add seam allowances to the templates. As you trace around the templates on your fabric, add ¼" (.6 cm) seam allowance around each piece. Cut out the pieces from the fabric.

All piecing is done with right sides of material facing and with seam allowances of ¼" (.6 cm). Iron seam allowances open after each new piece is added. To piece the Waterwheel Block (Figure 2):

1. Join Triangle 1 to Triangle 2 on their short sides to make a pieced triangle (Figure 3). Make three more pieced triangles in the same way. Set them aside.

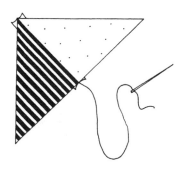

3. Join Triangle 1 to Triangle 2 on their short sides.

2. Take Square 5 and two of Rectangle 4. Attach a Rectangle 4 to the top of Square 5 and another Rectangle 4 to the bottom (Figure 4) to form a pieced rectangle.

3. Attach a Rectangle 3 to the left of the pieced rectangle you made in Step 2 (Figure 5). Attach another Rectangle 3 to the right side (Figure 6) to complete the center diamond shape.

4. Position the pieced triangles from Step 1 around the center diamond you made in Step 3 (Figure 7).

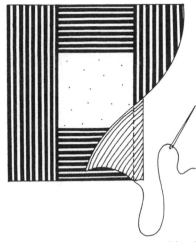

6. Attach a Rectangle 3 to the right side of the pieced rectangle.

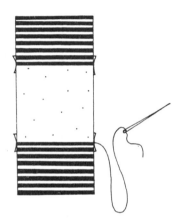

4. Attach a Rectangle 4 to the top and bottom of Square 5 to make a pieced rectangle.

7. Lay out the center diamond with the pieced triangles as shown.

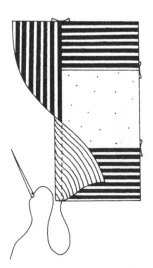

5. Attach a Rectangle 3 to the left side of the pieced rectangle.

5. Attach the pieced triangles you made in Step 2 to the center diamond (Figure 8) to complete the Waterwheel square.

6. Attach Rectangle 6 at the right side of the Waterwheel square (Figure 9).

7. Attach Rectangle 7 at the bottom to complete the Waterwheel Block (Figure 10).

8. Make as many Waterwheel blocks as you need for your quilt-top. Piece them as shown in Figure 1.

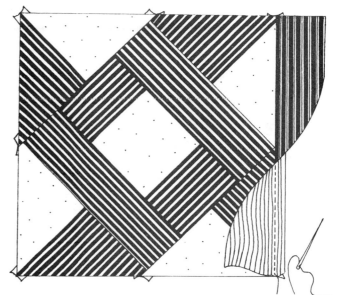

9. Attach Rectangle 6 at the right of the Waterwheel square.

8. Attach the pieced triangles to the center diamond to make the Waterwheel square.

10. Attach Rectangle 7 at the bottom to complete the Waterwheel Block.

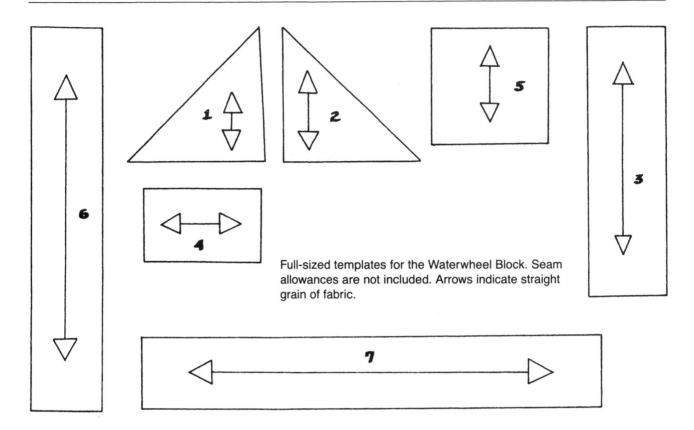

Full-sized templates for the Waterwheel Block. Seam allowances are not included. Arrows indicate straight grain of fabric.

Bow Tie

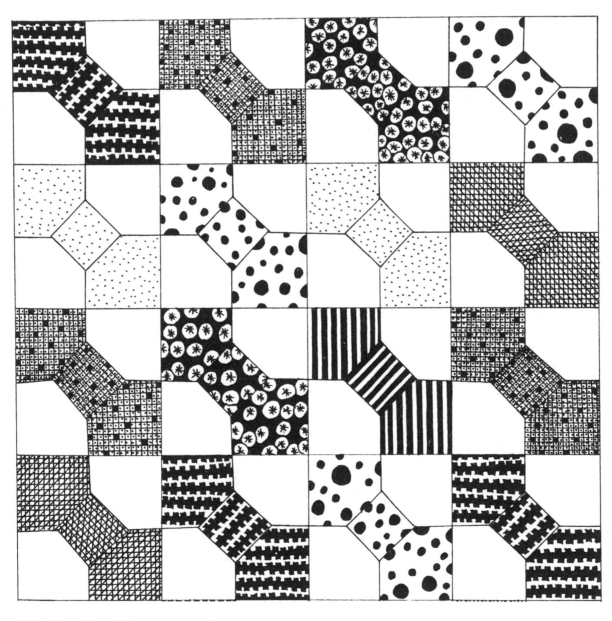

1. The Bow-Tie quilt-top.

Directions

Trace the template patterns onto template cardboard or plastic and cut out the templates. Do not add seam allowances to the templates. As you trace around the templates on your fabric, add ¼″ (.6 cm) seam allowance around each piece. Cut out the pieces from the fabric. To make the quilt-top shown in Figure 1, use a variety of patterned materials for pieces 1 and 2.

All piecing is done with right sides of material facing and with seam allowances of ¼″ (.6 cm). To piece the Bow Tie Block (Figure 2):

1. Join Piece 2 to Square 1 as shown in Figure 3.

2. Take Piece 3 and sew it to Piece 2 of the unit you made in Step 1 (Figure 4).

3. Join Piece 3 to Piece 1 (Figure 5) on the unit you made in Step 2.

4. Take a second Piece 2. Attach it to Piece 3 of the unit made in Step 3, as shown in Figure 6.

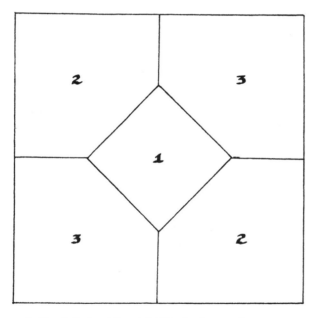

2. The full-sized Bow-Tie Block. Seam allowances are not included. Size: 3″ × 3″ (7.6 cm × 7.6 cm).

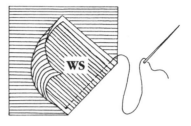

3. Join Piece 2 to Square 1.

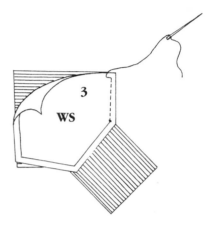

4. Join Piece 3 to Piece 2.

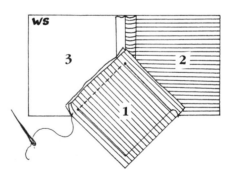

5. Attach Piece 3 to Piece 1.

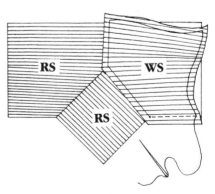

6. Attach Piece 2 to Piece 3.

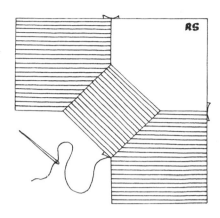

7. Attach Piece 1 to Piece 2.

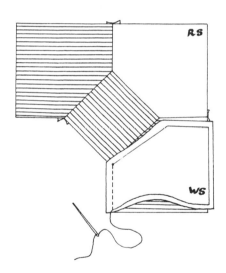

8. Attach Piece 3 to Piece 2.

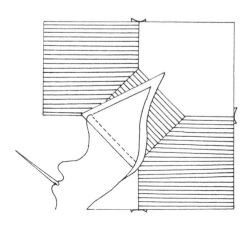

9. Attach Piece 3 to Piece 1.

5. Attach Piece 1 to Piece 2, as shown in Figure 7, on the unit made in Step 4.

6. Take another Piece 3 and attach it to Piece 2 on the unit from Step 5, as shown in Figure 8.

7. Attach the Piece 3 that you added in Step 6 to Piece 1, as shown in Figure 9.

8. Complete the block by joining the last seam, attaching Piece 3 to Piece 2 (Figure 10).

9. Make as many Bow-Tie blocks as you need for your quilt-top. Piece them as shown in Figure 1.

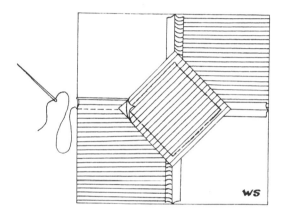

10. Attach Piece 2 to Piece 3 to complete the block.

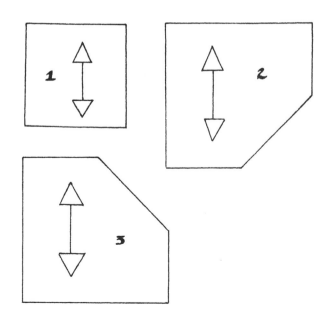

Full-sized templates for the Bow-Tie Block. Seam allowances are not included. Arrows indicate straight grain of fabric.

Spool

1. The Spool quilt-top.

Directions

Trace the template pattern onto template cardboard or plastic and cut out the template. Do not add seam allowances to the template. As you trace around the template on your fabric, add ¼″ (.6 cm) seam allowance around each piece. Cut out the pieces from the fabric. For each fabric piece you cut, also cut a paper pattern. Use the template to trace the paper patterns; however, do not add seam allowances to the paper patterns.

1. Notch the curved areas of each spool piece (Figure 2).

2. Position a paper pattern on the wrong side of a fabric piece. With large running stitches, baste the seam allowances down around the paper on the wrong side of the fabric (Figure 3). The paper pattern stabilizes the fabric; it will be removed after the quilt-top is completed.

3. Prepare all the spool pieces you need to make your quilt-top as described in Step 2.

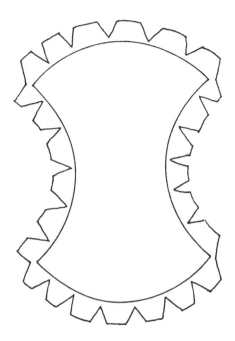

2. Notch the seam allowances of the Spool pieces.

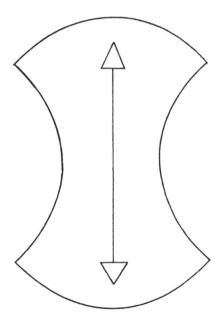

The full-sized template for the Spool quilt. Seam allowances are not included. Size: 3″ × 2″ (7.6 cm × 5.1 cm).

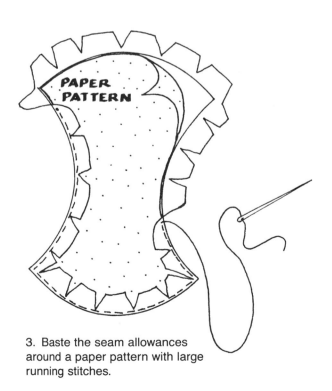

3. Baste the seam allowances around a paper pattern with large running stitches.

4. Stitch the spool pieces together with whipstitching (Figure 4), keeping your stitches small and even. Matching the color of the fabric and the thread will keep the stitches from showing too much. The concave ends of each patch will fit into the convex areas of other patches.

5. Iron the quilt-top when it is all pieced.

6. Remove the basting stitches, which also will release the paper patterns.

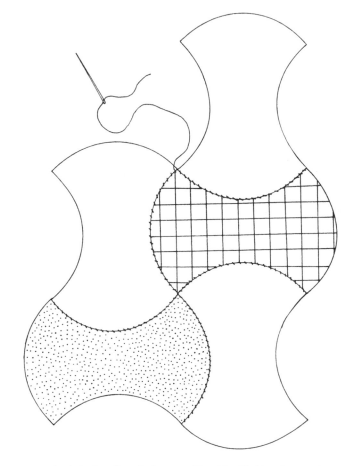

4. Join the Spool pieces with whipstitching to create the quilt-top.

Palm Leaves

1. The Palm Leaves quilt-top.

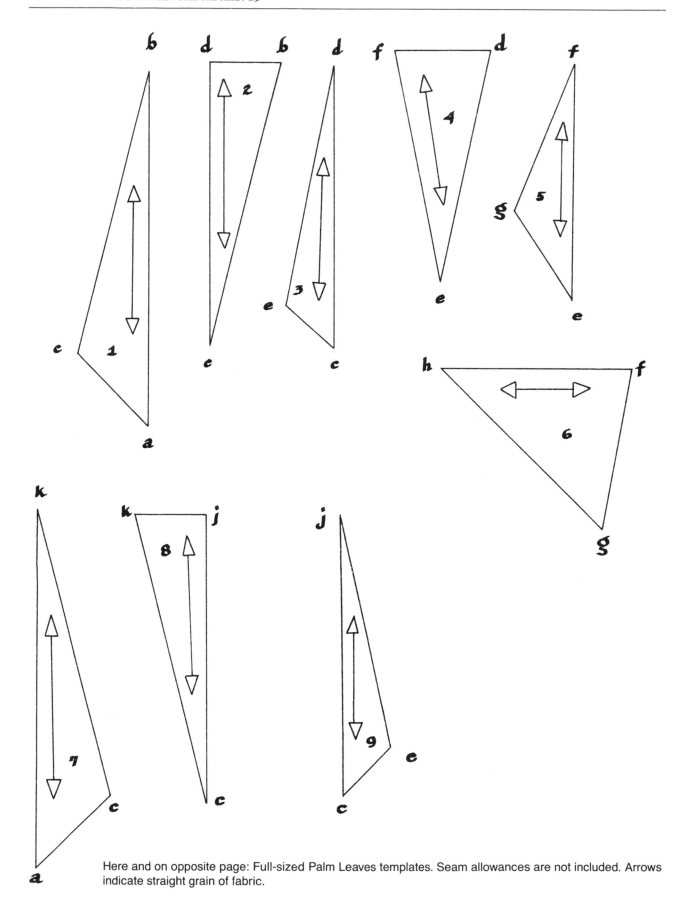

Here and on opposite page: Full-sized Palm Leaves templates. Seam allowances are not included. Arrows indicate straight grain of fabric.

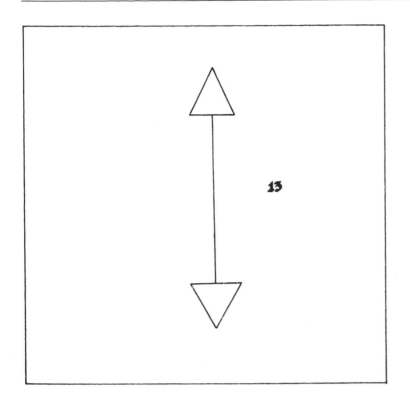

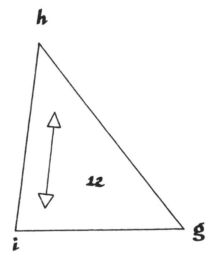

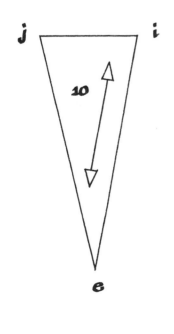

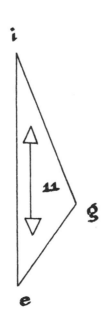

Directions

Trace the template patterns onto template cardboard or plastic and cut out the templates. Do not add seam allowances to the templates. As you trace around the templates on your fabric, add ¼″ (.6 cm) seam allowance around each piece. Cut out the pieces from the fabric.

All piecing is done with right sides of material facing and with seam allowances of ¼″ (.6 cm). Iron seam allowances open after each new piece is added. The Palm Leaves Block has two halves that are pieced triangles (see Figure 2).

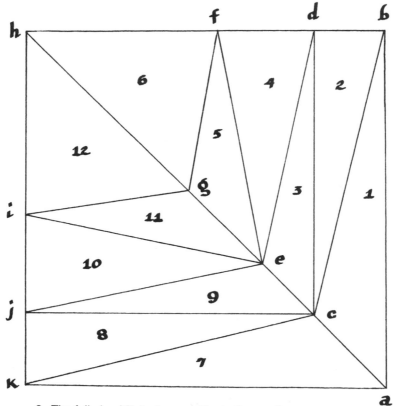

2. The full-sized Palm Leaves Block. Seam allowances are not included. Size: 3¾″ × 3¾″ (9.5 cm × 9.5 cm).

To piece the right half of the block:

1. Join Triangle 1 to Triangle 2 by sewing from b through c.

2. Attach Triangle 3 to the unit made in Step 2 by seaming Triangle 3 to Triangle 2 from d to c.

3. Attach Triangle 4 to the unit made in Step 2 by sewing Triangle 4 to Triangle 3 from d through e.

4. Attach Triangle 5 to the unit made in Step 3 by sewing it to Triangle 4 from f to e.

5. Attach Triangle 6 to the unit made in Step 4 by sewing it to Triangle 5 from f to g. This completes the right half of the Palm Leaves Block.

To piece the left half of the block, the same process is followed:

6. Sew Triangle 7 to Triangle 8 from k to c.

7. Sew Triangle 9 to the unit made in Step 6 by sewing it to Triangle 8 from j to c.

8. Sew Triangle 10 to the unit made in Step 7 by sewing it to Triangle 9 from j to e.

9. Sew Triangle 11 to the unit made in Step 8 by sewing it to Triangle 10 from i to e.

10. Sew Triangle 12 to the unit made in Step 9 by sewing it to Triangle 11 from i to g. This completes the left half of the Palm Leaf.

11. Join the right half and left half of the palm leaves by sewing from h to a (Figure 3). This completes the Palm Leaves block. Join solid Square 13 to the Palm Leaves Block (Figure 4).

12. Make as many blocks as you need for the quilt-top.

13. Join four blocks (two pieced, two solid) to form the quilt-top pattern (Figure 5). Make as many pattern units as you need to finish your quilt-top, joining them as shown in Figure 1.

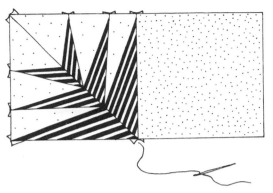

4. Join the Palm Leaves Blocks to solid squares to make the rows.

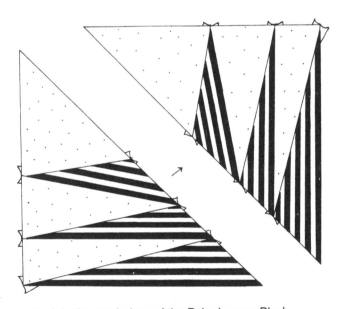

3. Join the two halves of the Palm Leaves Block.

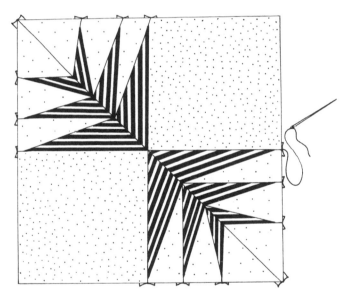

5. Join the rows as shown to make the quilt-top pattern.

Rosebud

1. The Rosebud quilt-top.

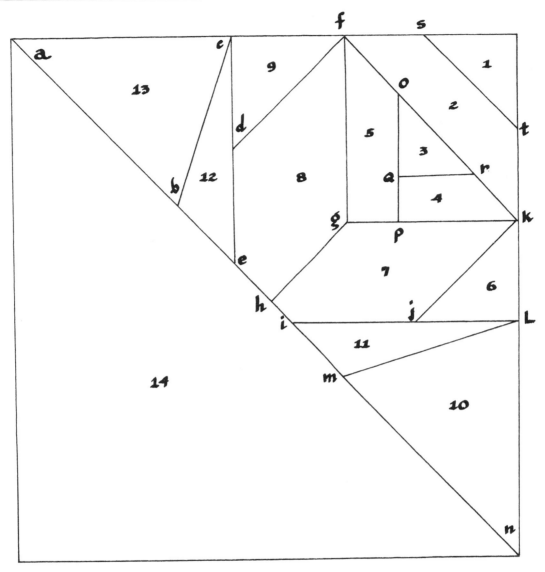

2. The full-sized Rosebud Block. Seam allowances are not included. Size: 5¼″ × 5½″ (13.3 cm × 14 cm).

Directions

Trace the template patterns onto template cardboard or plastic and cut out the templates. Do not add seam allowances to the templates. As you trace around the templates on your fabric, add ¼″ (.6 cm) seam allowance around each piece. Cut out the pieces from the fabric.

All piecing is done with right sides of material facing and with seam allowances of ¼″ (.6 cm). Iron seam allowances open after each new piece is added. The Rosebud Block consists of a large solid triangle and a large pieced triangle (Figure 2).

First we will make the large pieced triangle:

1. Sew Triangle 1 to Piece 2 from s to t (Figure 3). Set the unit aside.

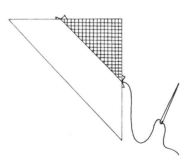

3. Sew Triangle 1 to Piece 2.

2. Sew Triangle 3 to Piece 4 from q to r (Figure 4).

3. Sew Piece 5 from p to o to the unit made in Step 2 (Figure 5). Set it aside.

4. Sew Piece 7 to Triangle 6 from j to k to form the right side of the bud (Figure 6).

5. Attach the right side of the bud, made in Step 4, to the pieced triangle made in Step 3 (Figure 7), sewing from g to k. Set it aside.

6. Form the left side of the bud by attaching Triangle 9 to Piece 8 by sewing from d to f (Figure 8).

7. Take the unit made in Step 5 and the unit made in Step 6. Attach them by sewing Piece 8 to Piece 7 from h to g (Figure 9). Cut off your stitches directly where the sewing lines meet.

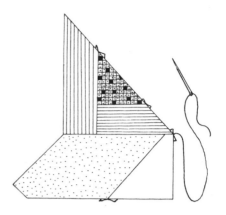

7. Attach the right side of the bud to the pieced triangle.

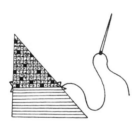

4. Sew Triangle 3 to Piece 4.

8. Seam Triangle 9 to Piece 8.

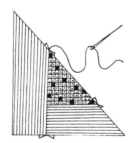

5. Attach Piece 5.

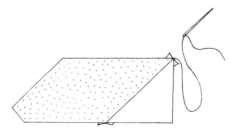

6. Sew Piece 7 to Triangle 6 to make the right side of the Rosebud.

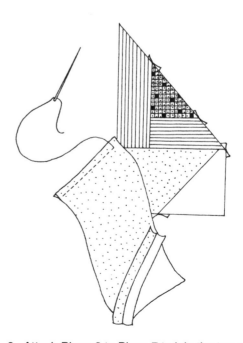

9. Attach Piece 8 to Piece 7 to join the two units.

8. Working with the same unit as in Step 7, sew from g to f to attach the left side of the Rosebud to the pieced triangle (Figure 10).

9. Add Triangle 11 to the unit pieced in Step 8 by sewing from i to L (Figure 11).

10. Attach Triangle 10 to the unit pieced in Step 9 by sewing from L to m (Figure 12).

11. Attach Triangle 12 to the unit pieced in Step 10 by sewing from c to e (Figure 13).

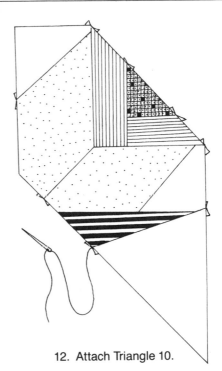

12. Attach Triangle 10.

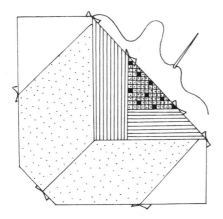

10. Join the left side of the Rosebud to the pieced triangle.

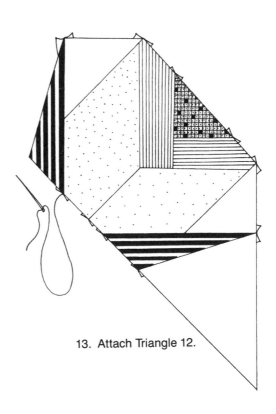

13. Attach Triangle 12.

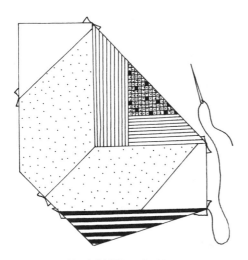

11. Add Triangle 11.

12. Attach Triangle 13 to the unit pieced in Step 11 by sewing from c to b (Figure 14).

13. Attach the unit made in Step 1 to the unit in Step 12 by sewing from f to k (Figure 15). This completes the large pieced triangle for the upper half of the Rosebud.

14. Attach Triangle 14 to the large pieced triangle by sewing from a through n (Figure 16). This completes the Rosebud Block.

15. Make as many Rosebud blocks as you need for your quilt-top. Join them as shown in Figure 1.

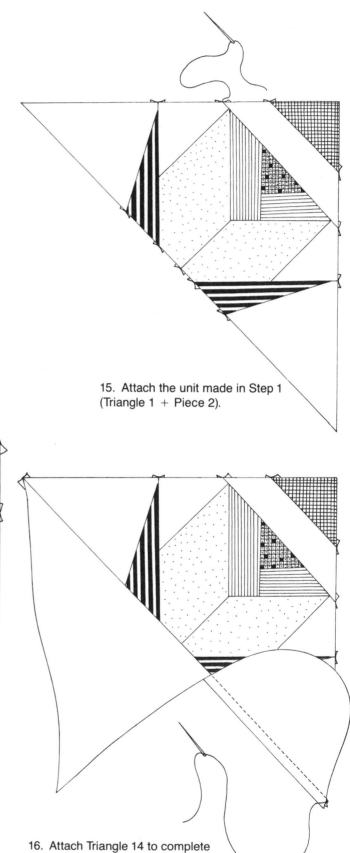

15. Attach the unit made in Step 1 (Triangle 1 + Piece 2).

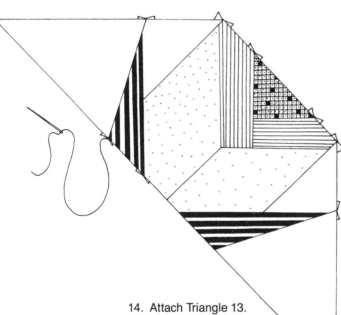

14. Attach Triangle 13.

16. Attach Triangle 14 to complete the Rosebud Block.

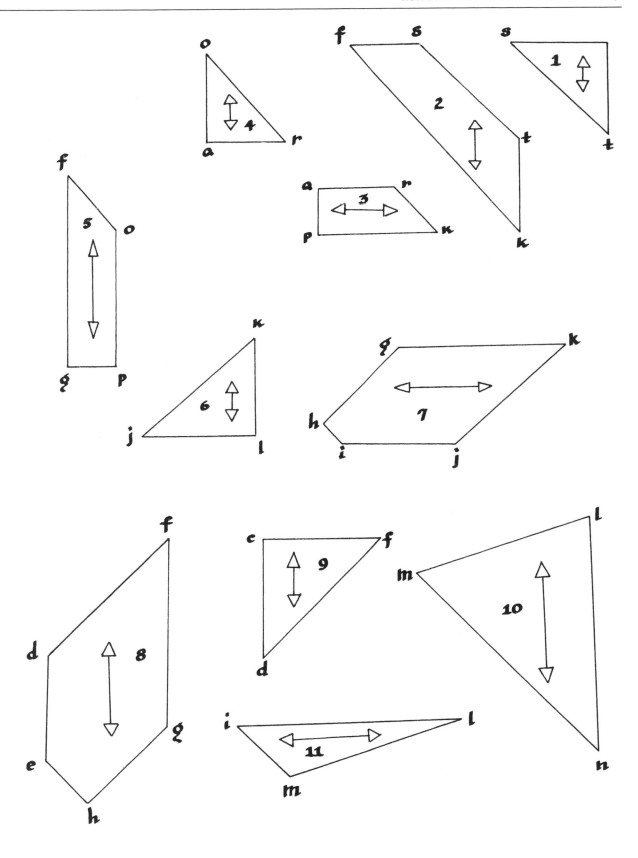

Here and next page: Full-sized Rosebud Block templates. Seam allowances are not included. Arrows indicate the straight grain of the fabric.

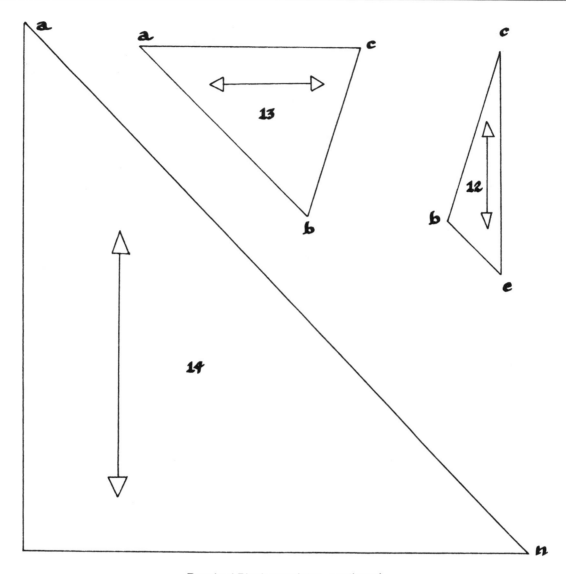

Rosebud Block templates, continued.

Scotty

1. The Scotty quilt-top.

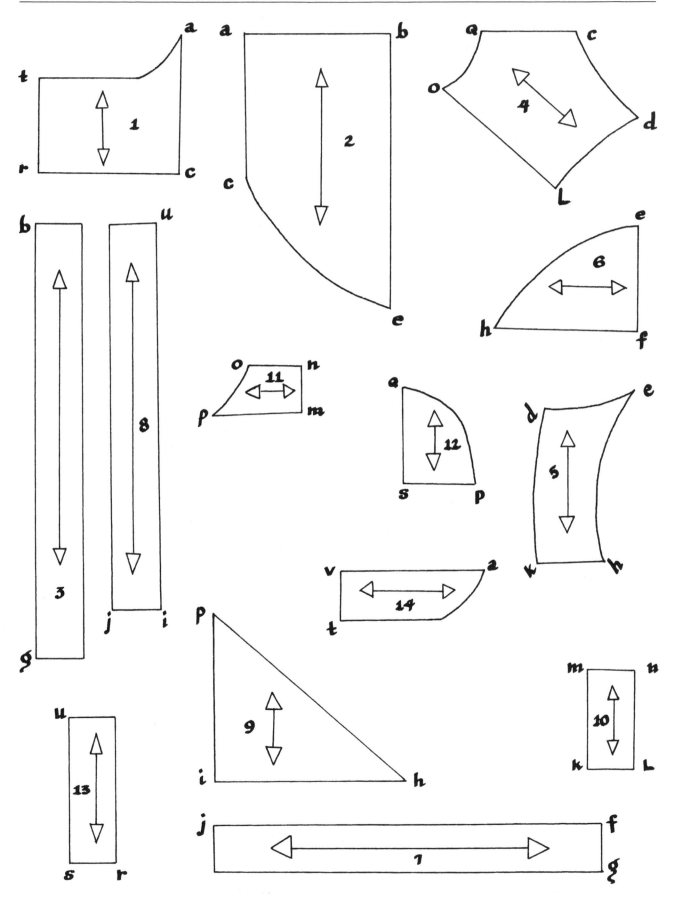

Full-sized templates for the Scotty Block. Seam allowances are not included. Arrows indicate straight grain of fabric.

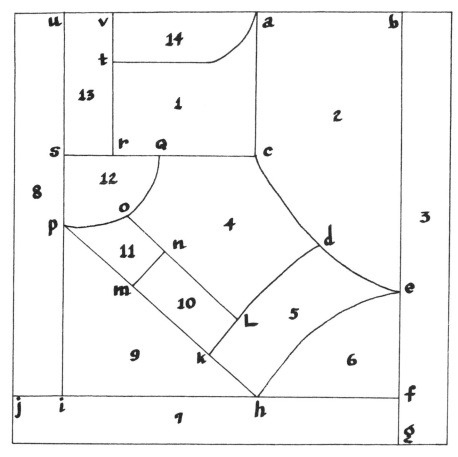

2. The full-sized Scotty Block. Seam allowances are not included. Size: 4½″ × 4½″ (11.4 cm × 11.4 cm).

Directions

Trace the template patterns onto template cardboard or plastic and cut out the templates. Do not add seam allowances to the templates. As you trace around the templates on your fabric, add ¼″ (.6 cm) seam allowance around each piece. Cut out the pieces from the fabric.

All piecing is done with right sides of material facing and with seam allowances of ¼″ (.6 cm). Iron seam allowances open after each new piece is added.

1. Sew Piece 1 to Piece 14 from t through a. Notch the curved areas (Figure 3) and iron the unit flat (Figure 4).

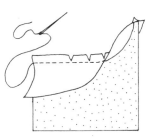

3. Attach Piece 14 to Piece 1. Notch the seams.

4. The unit of Piece 14 and Piece 1.

2. Attach Rectangle 13 to the unit you made in Step 1 by sewing from v through r (Figure 5). Set the unit aside.

3. Attach Piece 11 to Rectangle 10 by sewing from m to n (Figure 6).

4. Attach Piece 4 to the unit you made in Step 3 by sewing from o through L (Figure 7).

5. Attach Piece 12 to the unit made in step 4 by sewing from p to q. Notch the curved seam and iron the unit flat (Figure 8).

6. Attach Piece 5 to the unit made in step 5 by sewing from k to d (Figure 9).

7. Take the unit formed in Step 2 and the unit formed in Step 6 and join them by sewing from s to c (Figure 10).

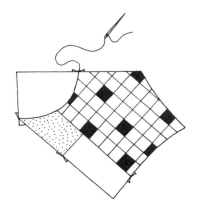

8. Attach Piece 12.

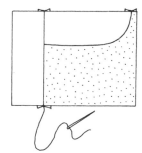

5. Attach Rectangle 13.

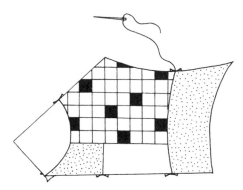

9. Attach Piece 5.

6. Attach Piece 11 to Rectangle 10.

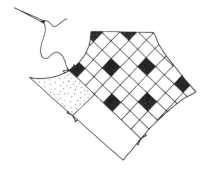

7. Attach Piece 4.

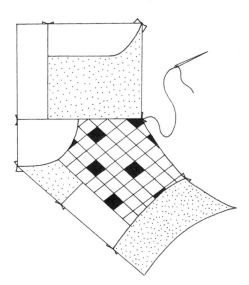

10. Join the two units.

8. Attach Piece 2 to the unit formed in Step 7, sewing from a through e (Figure 11). Notch the curved seam and iron the unit flat.

9. Attach Piece 6 to the unit formed in Step 8, sewing from e to h. (Figure 12). Notch the curved seam allowance and press the unit flat.

10. Attach Triangle 9 to the unit made in Step 9, sewing from p to h (Figure 13).

11. Attach Rectangle 8 to the unit made in Step 10, sewing from u to i (Figure 14).

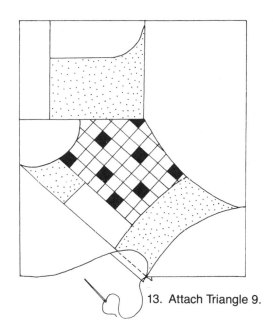

13. Attach Triangle 9.

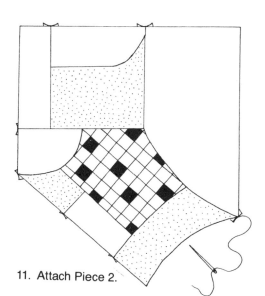

11. Attach Piece 2.

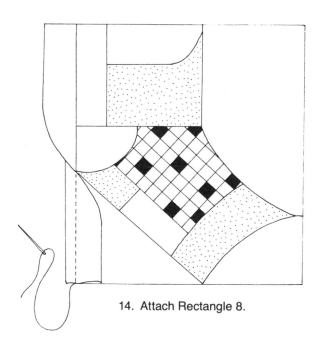

14. Attach Rectangle 8.

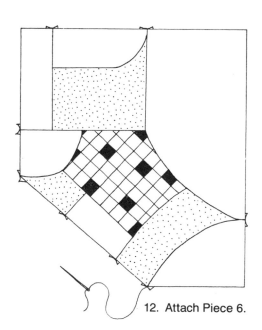

12. Attach Piece 6.

12. Attach Rectangle 7 to the unit formed in Step 11, sewing from j to f (Figure 15).

13. Attach Rectangle 3 to the unit formed in Step 12, sewing from b to g (Figure 16). This completes the Scotty Block.

14. Make as many Scotty blocks as you need for your quilt-top. Vary the patterned material used, if desired, for variety. Join the blocks into strips and then join the strips to make the quilt-top material (see Figure 1).

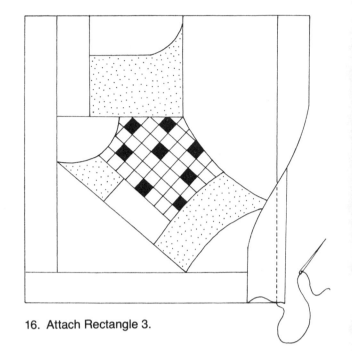

16. Attach Rectangle 3.

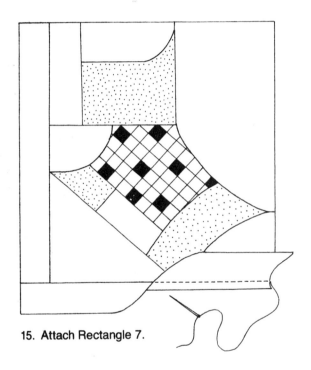

15. Attach Rectangle 7.

6
History of the Wearable Quilt

In Europe, the introduction of the quilt occurred during the Middle Ages with the return of the Crusaders from the wars. These early quilts were worn by knights and served as padding to protect the body from uncomfortable contact with the metal of their armor. Quilting had been used by the Persians at this time. Recent archaeological findings, however, indicate that quilting was used by the Chinese long before the time of the Crusades.

Simple Quilting

With the shift to a colder climate in medieval Europe, quilts became popular as bed coverlets and the craft of quilting flourished. In clothing, quilting was employed in vests, doublets, waistcoats and, most frequently, in petticoats.

During the Renaissance (1400–1600), quilting was employed in the stitching of the *busque*, an early Italian forerunner of the corset. Several layers of materials were quilted together to stiffen the body-encircling band. The *busque* was laced tightly at the back, giving the wearer a flat-chested appearance.

Quilted garments continued to be fashionable for both men and women, as may be seen in the clothing collection (circa 1620–1630), of the Victoria and Albert Museum in Great Britain. Early forms of wearable quilts had a single piece of cloth for the quilt-top, usually silk or linen. The batting was wool, and silk or linen was used for the backing. (Petticoats sometimes did not utilize batting, however.) Patterns formed by quilting stitches embellished the surface of early wearable quilts.

During the mid-18th century, the quilted petticoat was worn as an underskirt for a woman's gown. The gown, known as the *gown à l'anglaise*, was typically worn by wealthy English women and wealthy women of the American colonies (Figure 1). The softly gath-

1. *Gown à l'anglaise*, the gown at the height of fashion in 18th-century England, circa 1750.

217

ered skirt of the dress was worn open from the waist-line to the hem in front, exposing the elaborately quilted petticoat. The gown was fastened at the front with hidden hooks. The deep-cut neckline of the *gown à l'anglaise* was filled with a fichu.

The quilted petticoat was not sewn to the dress, but, rather, was a separate part of the ensemble. The quilted petticoat was pleated at the waist and sewn to a waistband which tied at the back. An oblong hoop, worn under the petticoat, gave the skirt a flattened appearance from the front and back views. Quilted petticoats were worn interchangeably with other dresses.

The practice of wearing quilted petticoats also filtered down to the less-than-wealthy women of the American colonies. Jonathan Holstein, in *The Pieced Quilt*, quotes from the diary of Ruth Henshaw Bascomb, an early quilter: "This afternoon twenty one ladies paid us a visit and assisted in quilting, on this occasion on Mrs. Henshaw's petticoat. It took four days, with some assistance, to prepare a quilt coat for Mrs. Scott."

Items for trade included petticoats. In 1753, the *Boston Evening Post* advertised the sale of petticoats as follows: "Women's Sarsnet Quilted Patticoats, 4 Yards Wide, Persian and Taminy Ditto. Long and Short Bone Hoop Petticoats."

Patchwork quilting, involving geometric and appliquéd piecing of the quilt-top, for which Americans are internationally known, was not widely utilized for clothing until the 1960s and 1970s, when self-expression in clothing became fashionable, as demonstrated by the popularity of ethnic clothing during these years.

2. Seminole patchwork skirt of commercial cotton cloth, Florida, circa 1940.

Seminole Patchwork

In the southeastern corner of the United States, around 1900, a different form of patchwork piecing evolved, known as Seminole Patchwork. The Seminole Indians of the Florida Everglades introduced a new technique of piecing fabrics for clothing applications.

The Seminole piecing technique involves the piecing of fabric units in a strip, utilizing light and dark colors to accentuate patterns. Strips are pieced together into a band. In addition to horizontal and vertical placement of the strips, strips sometimes are pieced together in an angled placement, to achieve a stair-stepped effect. Completed bands are pieced together to form the fabric (Figure 2). Seminole Patchwork offers limitless possibilities for clothing design applications.

3. A multi-colored Cuna Indian's mola blouse, circa 1980. Two reverse-appliquéd panels are sewn for the front and back sections of the bodice.

Reverse Appliqué

In South America, in the San Blas Islands off the coast of Panama, another form of patchwork piecing evolved, known as "reverse appliqué." Reverse appliqué is utilized by the Cuna Indians of Panama to embellish colorful blouses, shirts, and vests known as *molas* (Figure 3). The Cuna Indians' technique came to prominence around the early part of the 20th century. Historians speculate that the designs evolved from body painting, which was once fashionable among tribal members.

The Cuna Indians' method of reverse appliqué involves using several layers of fabrics and cutting the top ones to expose the colors of the underlayers. Another method reverses the process by building the layers, with the top layer applied last. All spaces in the surface of the quilt are filled with channelwork, from linear to circular patterns. Motifs formed by this method utilize bold designs of geometric, floral, and animal forms (Figure 4).

Among the waves of Asian immigration to the United States came the Hmong Tribe of Vietnam in the 1970s and 1980s, who brought an additional variation of the technique of reverse appliqué, known as *Pa Ndau* or flower cloth. In addition to geometric and curvilinear designs, embroidered motifs of flora and fauna also are utilized. In an often-used motif known as the "snail shell," small running stitches are worked into the channels (Figure 5). The snail shell represents the family. According to textile historian W. Porter-Francis (1987), the central motif of the snail shell represents the Hmong ancestors and the outer part of the shell, the successive generations. Life, death, and religion are represented in *Pa Ndau*.

A

B

4. Multicolored figurative motifs of Cuna Indians' molas, Panama, circa 1980.

Quilting Today

The blending of ethnic heritage and skills has brought about a richness and variety in quilts. Like the quilted coverlet, quilted clothing also is steadily gaining in popularity. Unique visual effects, made possible by various forms of patchwork techniques, have attracted a new wave of clothing designers in the world of fashion.

Today, quilting has attained international recognition as a time-honored skill. Hand-pieced quilted coverlets and clothing are coveted worldwide for their aesthetic appeal as well as for their value. The unique quality of quilting as a functional art of self-expression has assured its place in the realm of decorative and fine arts.

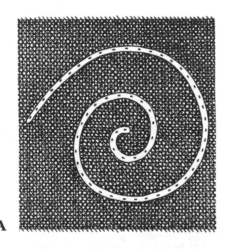

A

B

5.   A: The Hmong snail shell motif. The snail shell motif represents the family; the inner coil symbolizes the ancestors, the outer part of the coil symbolizes the successive generations.   B: The double snail-shell motif symbolizes the union of two families.

BIBLIOGRAPHY

Avery, V. *The Big Book of Appliqué*, New York: Charles Scribner's Sons, 1978.

Bigelow, M. *Fashion In History*, New York: Macmillan Publishing Co., 1979.

Brackman, B. How to treat quilts tenderly, *Americana, 13* (3), 68–70, 1985.

Colby, A. *Quilting*. New York: Charles Scribner's Sons, 1971.

Conn, R. *Native American Art in the Denver Museum*. Seattle: University of Washington Press, 1979.

Dudley, T. *Strip Patchwork*. New York: Van Nostrand Reinhold Co., 1980.

Earle, A. *Costume of Colonial Times*. New York. Charles Scribner's Sons, 1894.

Editors of Consumer Guide. *Patchwork Quilts*. New York: Beckman House, 1982.

Hillhouse, M., and E. Mansfield. *Dress Design and Flat Pattern Making*. Boston: Houghton Mifflin Co., 1948.

Holstein, J. *American Pieced Quilts*. New York: Avon Books, 1972.

Holstein, J. *The Pieced Quilt: An American Tradition*. New York: Galahad Books, 1973.

Ickis, M. *The Standard Book of Quilt Making and Collecting*. New York: Dover Publications, Inc., 1959.

The Illustrated Encyclopedia of Costume and Fashion: 1550–1920. London: Blandford Press, 1971.

Joseph, M. *Introductory Textile Science*. New York: CBS College Publishing, 1986.

Kelley, F., and R. Schwabe. *Historic Costume*. London: Morrison and Gibb Ltd., 1925.

Nelson, C., and C. Houck. *Treasury of American Quilts*. New York: Greenwich House, 1982.

Patera, C. The Kunas Revisited, *Quilt*, 22–25, 1984 (winter).

Porter-Francis, W. A flourishing art: USA, *Threads Magazine*, 33–37, 1987, February/March.

Riggs, C., and J. Sherill. *Textile Laundering Technology*. Florida: Textile Rental Services Association of America, 1979.

Weeks, L., and J. Christensen. *Quilting: Patchwork and Trapunto*. New York: Sterling Publishing Co., Inc., 1980.

ABOUT THE AUTHOR

Roselyn Gadia-Smitley is a graduate of Texas Women's University with a doctorate degree in textiles and clothing. She received her bachelor of arts and master of arts from California State University, Los Angeles, in textiles and clothing. Her areas of study have been primarily clothing construction, textiles science, interior design, art, fashion design, and fashion merchandising.

The author is presently a faculty member of New Mexico State University. She holds a lifetime teaching credential for community colleges in the state of California for textiles, clothing, and related technologies. She is affiliated with the American Home Economics Association (AHEA), the American Collegiate Retailing Association (ACRA), The Costume Society of America (CSA), and the International Textile and Apparel Association (ITAA). Her published works include the *Dolls' Clothes Pattern Book*, also published by Sterling Publishing Co., Inc.

METRIC EQUIVALENCY CHART

MM—MILLIMETRES   CM—CENTIMETRES

INCHES TO MILLIMETRES AND CENTIMETRES

INCHES	MM	CM	INCHES	CM	INCHES	CM
⅛	3	0.3	9	22.9	30	76.2
¼	6	0.6	10	25.4	31	78.7
⅜	10	1.0	11	27.9	32	81.3
½	13	1.3	12	30.5	33	83.8
⅝	16	1.6	13	33.0	34	86.4
¾	19	1.9	14	35.6	35	88.9
⅞	22	2.2	15	38.1	36	91.4
1	25	2.5	16	40.6	37	94.0
1¼	32	3.2	17	43.2	38	96.5
1½	38	3.8	18	45.7	39	99.1
1¾	44	4.4	19	48.3	40	101.6
2	51	5.1	20	50.8	41	104.1
2½	64	6.4	21	53.3	42	106.7
3	76	7.6	22	55.9	43	109.2
3½	89	8.9	23	58.4	44	111.8
4	102	10.2	24	61.0	45	114.3
4½	114	11.4	25	63.5	46	116.8
5	127	12.7	26	66.0	47	119.4
6	152	15.2	27	68.6	48	121.9
7	178	17.8	28	71.1	49	124.5
8	203	20.3	29	73.7	50	127.0

YARDS TO METRES

YARDS	METRES	YARDS	METRES	YARDS	METRES	YARDS	METRES	YARDS	METRES
⅛	0.11	2⅛	1.94	4⅛	3.77	6⅛	5.60	8⅛	7.43
¼	0.23	2¼	2.06	4¼	3.89	6¼	5.72	8¼	7.54
⅜	0.34	2⅜	2.17	4⅜	4.00	6⅜	5.83	8⅜	7.66
½	0.46	2½	2.29	4½	4.11	6½	5.94	8½	7.77
⅝	0.57	2⅝	2.40	4⅝	4.23	6⅝	6.06	8⅝	7.89
¾	0.69	2¾	2.51	4¾	4.34	6¾	6.17	8¾	8.00
⅞	0.80	2⅞	2.63	4⅞	4.46	6⅞	6.29	8⅞	8.12
1	0.91	3	2.74	5	4.57	7	6.40	9	8.23
1⅛	1.03	3⅛	2.86	5⅛	4.69	7⅛	6.52	9⅛	8.34
1¼	1.14	3¼	2.97	5¼	4.80	7¼	6.63	9¼	8.46
1⅜	1.26	3⅜	3.09	5⅜	4.91	7⅜	6.74	9⅜	8.57
1½	1.37	3½	3.20	5½	5.03	7½	6.86	9½	8.69
1⅝	1.49	3⅝	3.31	5⅝	5.14	7⅝	6.97	9⅝	8.80
1¾	1.60	3¾	3.43	5¾	5.26	7¾	7.09	9¾	8.92
1⅞	1.71	3⅞	3.54	5⅞	5.37	7⅞	7.20	9⅞	9.03
2	1.83	4	3.66	6	5.49	8	7.32	10	9.14

INDEX